leisure activities for the mature adult

Joan M. Moran

Texas Woman's University

 **Burgess Publishing Company**
Minneapolis, Minnesota

Editor: Wayne Schotanus
Production Manager: Morris Lundin
Art Director: Joan Gordon
Designer: Mari Ansari
Artist: Barbara Warrington
Sales/Marketing Manager: Travis Williams

Photographs courtesy of the Edina Care Center (photographs by Mari Ansari
and Paula Gibbons) and the Richfield Community Center.

FOREWORD

Programming for the leisure needs of the aged is not a new phenomenon, but it is one which has been given limited priority in our society. Because this segment of our population is rapidly increasing, the need for quality social and recreational activity programs designed to attain and maintain the quality of life of the aged, whom Joan so aptly calls "mature adults," is great. The concept of sustaining the same rhythm and routine of normal life patterns has long been recognized as an essential element in this maintenance of a high quality of life in the years after retirement. This normal life rhythm and routine can be best attained in the years after retirement if purposeful, enjoyable activity is substituted for the work-type activities performed in the preretirement years. Social and recreational activity, therefore, is basic in the hierarchy of needs of the retiree. This text contains a broad range and variety of social and recreational activities which will enhance the life of all retirees regardless of their abilities, needs, interests, or aspirations.

In 1975 the Older Americans Act was amended to broaden the definition of social services to include "services designed to enable older persons to attain and maintain physical and mental well-being through programs of regular activity and exercise." The chapter in this text on Sports and Exercise includes a wide range of mild, moderate, and vigorous activities, with appropriate precautionary measures stressing the health and safety of the participant. These materials will provide the recreation leader with the sound programming guidelines needed to assist the aged individual in developing fitness through exercise, an aspect vitally needed by this segment of our population as a preventive-medicine approach to a healthy, enjoyable retirement period.

A frequently overlooked and untapped quality of the aged is their creative skill and potential. Numerous suggestions, which may facilitate the release of creative abilities in all of the various art forms, have been included throughout the text. In fact, structured art and craft activities that have been included, involve or lend themselves to the release of the creative abilities of the participants.

Leadership is a critical aspect of sound recreational programming and means more than qualified professional staff and volunteers. Only when the older participants, themselves, are actively involved in both the planning and leadership of their social and recreational activity program will such programs be successful and effective. This type of participant involvement is essential in all types of programs in the community and in extended-care facilities. The author has aptly addressed these concerns and has provided sound principles and guidelines for effective programming, including evaluation procedures essential to the attainment and maintenance of quality social and recreational activity programming for retirees.

Social and recreational activity is basic in the hierarchy of needs of retirees if they are to maintain a high quality of life. The reader of this text will find numerous ideas and techniques basic to the effective development and implementation of quality programs of "Leisure Activities for the Mature Adult."

William A. Hillman, Jr., Past President
National Therapeutic Recreation Society

March 1977

PREFACE

The title *Leisure Activities for the Mature Adult* reflects the author's belief that growing old is not the same as being old and that chronological age is a wholly unworthy and very poor criterion to use as an arbitrary dividing line between middle and old age. That segment of our population 55-65 years of age and older is a very heterogeneous group. In fact, many of these individuals are not aged.

Early retirement and a healthier older population indicate that recreation programs for this segment of our population should include a variety of activities ranging in intensity from moderate through vigorous, if the diverse needs of all mature adults are to be met. Such well-rounded programs should provide an outlet for physical, mental, and social energies and interests. To make this type of programming possible, the recreation-program activity director should be encouraged to secure proper medical releases on all participants so that vigorous, moderate, and mild sports and exercise can be an integral part of this total recreation program. Participant involvement in the actual planning and implementation of the activity program is also a critically important element if a program is to be successful.

One of the best ways to stay well and happy after 40 and into the later years of life is to develop new interests and make new friends. The "will to live" can be a significant factor in determining how rapidly people recover from major illness or even in whether such illnesses develop. As an active participant in the mainstream of life, the retiree will remain intellectually alert and socially assertive and will be engaged with the environment and other people. Recreation can be an extremely important aid to growing old gracefully and fostering positive attitudes toward an active interest in living.

Because an understanding of the biological/physiological, psychological, and sociological aspects of aging is necessary for the specialist working in recreation programs for mature adults, background information on these subjects is included in the text. Although discussed separately, it should be remembered that a human is a total biological/physiological, psychological, and sociological being and that these aspects of life interact and are constantly changing and evolving to produce a unique person. It should also be stressed that mental and emotional deterioration and decline are not inevitable by-products of advanced age.

Because many mature adults may suffer from various kinds and degrees of handicapping conditions, suggestions for working with the handicapped mature adult are included throughout the text.

It is hoped that, if the recreation director thinks of this segment of our population as mature adults with varied talents and potential, a more creative, active recreation program will evolve and less time will be devoted to "childlike activities." Thus, the quality of life of the older segment of our population will improve as these members of our society become actively involved in enjoyable, creative, worthwhile activity and make such activity a part of their everyday lives.

Aging is one circumstance of life that affects every individual, and growing old will be the fate of all those privileged to live seven or more decades. When this happens to you, will you want to be called old, or a mature adult?

January 1977   Joan May Moran

CONTENTS

*To Mom,
and all of my relatives and
friends who are growing old
gracefully, this book is
dedicated.*

1
THE AGING PROCESS—
A STATISTICAL OVERVIEW

A long life is needed to become young.
— Picasso, 91 years

Aging is not a disease or a disintegrative force, but, rather, it is a process of changes, involving all aspects of the human organism, which becomes more accelerated in the middle years of life. Although the process of aging is eventually evident in everyone, aging is a continuous process which does not progress at an even rate. Those individuals 55-65 years of age and older are a very heterogeneous group. It can even be said that many of them are not aged.

Considerable discrepancies exist between and within individuals in the rate and degree of change in the structure and function of component tissues of the human body and the altered relationships of the organism to its physical and social environments. It is impossible to establish a definite age in the average life span at which all members of the human race can be classified as "old" and in need of special services. The chronological age of a person, therefore, is a wholly unworthy and very poor criterion to use as an arbitrary dividing line between middle and old age. An individual's physiological, sociological, psychological, and intellectual levels of functioning, in addition to that person's life-style and life patterns, must be used as the criteria for establishing this dividing line between middle and old age.

Increased knowledge and control of bacterial and parasitic diseases, a clearer understanding of human nutrition, better health care, better living conditions, and other advances in preventive medicine have all contributed to a greater life expectancy and have, in many cases, even slowed the aging process. When humanity learned to control the environment, especially sanitation, famine, and

1

pestilence, the mortality rate was greatly reduced, thus contributing to an increase in life expectancy.

According to the Federal Security Agency (HEW, 1955):

> *Since 1900, the population of the United States has doubled, but the number of persons forty-five to sixty-four years has tripled, while the number sixty-five years and older has quadrupled. There are now (early 1952) thirteen million men and women sixty-five years of age and over. This number is increasing currently at the rate of about four hundred thousand a year. Between 1940 and 1950 the country's population sixty-five years and over went up 36%. One in every twelve persons in the country is sixty-five years and over. . . . Women out-number men ten to nine in the sixty-five and over age group. More than half of the women in this age class are widows. The majority of the men sixty-five years and over and still married, on the other hand.*

A comparison of the average life span of men and women in the 1970s with that of prior generations clearly verifies this trend toward increased longevity.

CHANGES IN LIFE EXPECTANCY

Century	Average Life Expectancy	Extended Life Expectancy
Sixteenth	21	
Seventeenth	26	
Eighteenth	35	
Nineteenth	40	
Twentieth	68	
1900	47.3 (U.S.)	Male 46.3, Female 48.3 (U.S.)
1940	49.2 (U.S.)	
1951	68.5 (U.S.)	Male 65.9, Female 71.8 (U.S.)
1954	69.6 (U.S.)	
1967	70.5 (U.S.)	Male 67, Female 74.2 (U.S.)
1970	70.7 (U.S.)	Male 67, Female 74.3 (U.S.)
1971	70.8 (U.S.)	
1973	71.3 (U.S.)	
1974	71.9 (U.S.)	Male 68.1, Female 75.8 (U.S.)
	73.3 (Japan)	
	53.9 (West Africa, Polynesia, other less developed regions)	
2000 (estimates)	75-80 (developing countries)	
	60-65 (third world countries)	

Compiled from statistical data—United Nations Reports, World Health Organization, Metropolitan Life Insurance Company.

POPULATION OF UNITED STATES BY AGE AND SEX
PERCENT DISTRIBUTION

Age Interval	1950 M	1950 F	1960 M	1960 F	1970 M	1970 F
Under 5	11.01	10.45	11.69	10.98	8.75	8.08
5-9	8.97	8.55	10.76	10.10	10.17	9.39
10-14	7.56	7.20	9.65	9.07	10.59	9.78
15-19	7.10	6.99	7.51	7.24	9.74	9.05
20-24	7.48	7.74	5.97	6.08	8.56	8.09
25-29	7.98	8.27	6.04	6.08	6.79	6.61
30-34	7.52	7.77	6.62	6.71	5.66	5.56
35-39	7.37	7.55	6.88	7.04	5.51	5.48
40-44	6.78	6.77	6.43	6.51	5.82	5.88
45-49	6.05	5.99	6.07	6.05	5.92	6.03
50-54	5.52	5.46	5.36	5.35	5.29	5.49
55-59	4.85	4.75	4.67	4.73	4.76	4.99
60-64	4.06	3.98	3.86	4.10	4.03	4.40
65-69	3.24	3.40	3.32	3.66	3.06	3.59
70-74	2.18	2.35	2.47	2.81	2.37	3.12
75 & Over	2.33	2.78	2.70	3.49	2.98	4.46

Compiled from data contained in the July 1972 Utah Public Health Profile, Utah Center for Health Statistics, Utah State Division of Health, Salt Lake City, Utah.

POPULATION OVER AGE 65

Year	% Population over 65	Population over 65
1900	4.1%	3 million
1920		5 million
1940		9 million
1952	8.4%	13 million
1960		17 million
1970	10.2%	20 million
1974		22 million
2000 (estimates)		28.2 - 30 million

U.S. Census Bureau

Between 1960 and 1965 there was a 9 percent increase in the number of persons in the 65-years-and-older age group in the United States. According to population experts, during an average day 3900 persons reach the age of 65 (1.4 million annually), and 3080 persons over 65 years of age die (1.1 million annually). Thus, there is an average daily net increase of 820 persons in the 65-years-and-older age group, or approximately 301,000 annually. It is estimated that by the year 2000 between 45 and 50 million middle-aged adults will have reached their 65th birthday.

Since the turn of the century, the population of the United States has tripled, surpassing the 200 million figure (207,237,000). But the population of persons 65 years and older has grown seven times as large (22 million or 10 percent of the total population). And this population of senior citizens is getting older (approximately 37 percent are over the age of 75).

1970 U.S. CENSUS

Number of Americans	Age in Years
22 million	65 and over
10 million	73 and over
1 million	85 and over
106 thousand	100 and over

Statistics available in the state of Utah indicate that, in 1960, 4 percent or 11,000 persons were 65 or older. In 1975 this figure had jumped to 7½ percent or 88,000 persons 65 or older. This population increase in senior citizens is typical of national trends and reflects the increases in life expectancy brought about by a 2 percent decrease in death rate from heart disease, a 5 percent decline in stroke rate, and a 20 percent drop in death rate from auto accidents (Metropolitan Life Insurance Co. 1975).

It is estimated that between 1960 and 1985 the aged population of the United States will increase 50 percent and the group 85 years and older may nearly double. In 1970 half of the 20 million individuals over age 65 were under 73 and more than a million were 85 or older. It is estimated that the number of individuals 75 and older will continue to increase at about twice the rate of the over-65 group as a whole and at more than twice the rate of the total population.

Life expectancy at age 65 is approximately 15 years (13 years for men, 16 years for women). In 1900 it was 11 years for men and 12 years for women. According to the U.S. Census Bureau, in 1974 cancer and diseases of the circulatory and nervous systems were the leading causes of death in advanced age in developing nations in the world. If major medical breakthroughs occur in the treatment of these diseases, we can anticipate a tremendous increase in life expectancy at age 65. Some estimates go as high as 31 years, which would make the average life span 96 years.

GENETIC AND ENVIRONMENTAL FACTORS AFFECTING LONGEVITY

Numerous individual characteristics and environmental conditions affect or directly or indirectly influence longevity. According to authorities on aging, the most influential factors are heredity, sex, race, environment, family and life patterns, and education.

Heredity

Research evidence tends to indicate that longevity is hereditary. An individual's genetic inheritance affects the aging process by passing on deficiencies or the predisposition for certain diseases. Heredity also helps determine one's ability to adapt to life's stresses. Naturally, accidents and serious illness can adversely affect the life expectancy of some members in a family with a predisposition for longevity.

Sex

Since the time of the ancient Romans, the statistics of aging have revealed significant evidence that women generally outlive men.

COMPARATIVE LONGEVITY OF MEN TO WOMEN

Year	Over Age 65 Ratio Males to Females	
1900	94	100
1952	85.7	100
1970	72	100
1974	70	100

In the older population women currently outnumber men by over three million. This ratio increases significantly with age.

Age	Males	Females
65-69	100	120
85+	100	160

It is estimated that by 1985 there will be 40 percent more women than men in this older age group. This difference between the sexes in aging and longevity is directly related to the role women play in society. The female role usually is safer, less strenuous or stressful (it is believed that women can handle the stresses of everyday life better than men), less adventuresome and, therefore, less accident-prone. Women as a group have a smaller incidence of high blood pressure and heart trouble. The twentiety-century liberalization of the female and its potential for role change might adversely affect this domination by the female of aging statistics in modern society.

Race

Members of the white race have a greater life expectancy than members of the nonwhite races. White persons make up less than 90 percent of the total population but 92 percent of the older population. This may be partially based on the fact that nearly twice as many nonwhites as whites 65 years or older dwell in poverty or live in substandard housing. Hopefully, the new civil rights laws will eliminate this racial difference in longevity.

RACIAL DIFFERENCES IN LONGEVITY

Race	Life Expectancy—1970	
	Female	Male
White	73.6	67.4
Nonwhite	65.8	61.0

Environment

Life expectancy is greater in urban than in rural areas and in the Western United States than in the Central United States. Only 1.3 million or just under 10 percent of the farm population is 65 and over. Nearly 9 million individuals 65 and over, however, are living in rural areas and small towns. This represents 41 percent of the population of the United States. One-third of the elderly in rural areas live in poverty compared with 25 percent in central cities and 17 percent in suburban areas. It is anticipated that future generations of older citizens will join the major trend toward urbanization. Many of them will live in the central city, not because of convenience, but rather because the central city will become more and more the locus of the poor.

Family and Life Pattern

The mortality rate is greater for single and divorced persons than for married persons. This, however, is more true for men than women. Persons from large families, especially older siblings, tend to outlive those from small families or those born to older parents primarily because they have learned those adaptive skills that enable them to face the stresses of life better. Seven of every 10 older persons live in families; about a quarter live alone or with nonrelatives. Only 1 in 25 (4 percent or approximately 1.5 million) lives in an institution such as a nursing home, hospital, home for the aged, or mental institution. Three times as many older women as older men live alone or with nonrelatives. Thus, an overwhelming majority of the aged population live with varying degrees of self-sufficiency, yet independently in the community.

Educational Attainment

The higher the educational level of the individual, the greater his or her chances are to live a long life. Because those with better education usually go into vocations with greater financial remuneration, there is a relationship between longevity and occupation. However, stress at higher vocational levels can influence longevity. Statistics indicate that half of the people over 65 today had only elementary schooling or less; at least half of those under 65 years of age today have had some high school education. Approximately 5 percent of our senior citizens are college graduates, with 2.4 million having had at least some college education. Of every 100 older people, a total of 8 men and 8 women 65 years old and above have had none or less than 5 years of school and are functionally illiterate (approximately a million or 16.6 percent of the elderly). About 20 percent of today's 65-and-over population are foreign born, which may account for their lack of formal education. The present compulsory public-education legislation to age 16 will significantly alter the educational level of future senior citizens.

SECONDARY FACTORS THAT INFLUENCE LONGEVITY

Other less direct factors that affect aging and longevity are economic level, employment after age 65, political power, medical care, and chronic disabling conditions.

Economic Level

Older families average just under 50 percent of the income of younger families; older persons living alone or with nonrelatives average only 40 percent of the income of their younger counterparts. In 1968 about 25 percent of all older persons were living in households with incomes below the poverty line for that type and size of family. Almost 30 percent of the older families had incomes of less than $3,000 in 1968; more than 40 percent of the older people living alone or with nonrelatives had incomes of less than $1,500. In contrast, about 10 percent had incomes of at least $10,000 and less than 1 percent (a total of 75,000 families) had $25,000 a year or more.

Labor Force Participation

In 1900 about 66.6 percent of the men 65 and older were in the labor market, in contrast to approximately 25 percent in 1970. Rates for females increased from about 8 percent in 1900 to almost 10 percent in 1970. The rate drops sharply after age 70. Between ages 65 and 69, 42.3 percent of the males and 17.3 percent of the females are in the labor market. After age 70, only 18 percent of the males and 6.1 percent of the females are working. This reduction can be directly attributed to our highly technological society and its accent on youth.

Employment comprises the largest single source of the $45 billion income of the elderly. This, however, represents a source for only approximately 20 percent of this older population. Regular retirement programs contribute about 40 percent of total income, with 30 percent coming from Social Security, 6 percent from railroad retirement and civil service, and 3 percent from private pension plans. In addition, about 40 percent comes from veterans' benefits and 5 percent from public assistance. In summary, 45 percent of the total income of our aged population comes from retirement payments of one sort or another.

Political Power

The political power of the elderly has the potential for significant growth. At the present time they represent about 15 percent of the eligible voters. In the future they will approximate 25 percent, even if the improvements in life expectancy as a result of conquering major killers do not occur.

Medical Care

Persons over 65 have 1 chance in 7 of requiring short-term hospital care, and 1 in 25 of requiring long-term care in any one year. The chances for long-term care increase with age. While only 1 in 50 of those between 65 and 72 requires long-term care, 1 in 15 of those 73 and over requires this care. Older people suffer more disabilities than the general population, visit their physicians more often, and, as one might expect, spend more time in the hospital. Yet about 83 percent of the elderly get along on their own. According to Sen. Frank Moss (D., Utah), chairman of the President's Committee on Aging, Medicare covers only 40 percent of the medical needs of the elderly. In addition, a drastic need currently exists for medical and dental care for low-income elderly. This statement is based on the fact that 20 percent of the elderly in the state of Utah do not currently receive necessary medical and dental care.

Chronic Conditions and Mobility

According to the U.S. Department of Health, Education and Welfare (1970), chronic conditions are conditions of impairments that have lasted for more than three months or those with a more recent onset which appear on lists of medically determined, long-lasting conditions. They range from visual impairments corrected by eyeglasses to completely disabling strokes. Typical chronic conditions include: arthritis and rheumatism, diabetes, heart disease, high blood pressure and other cardiovascular ailments, mental and nervous conditions, hearing impairments, and visual problems. Approximately 75 percent of the aged 65-74 and 80 percent of the aged over age 75 suffer from one or more chronic conditions as compared to 40 percent under age 65.

In most cases, chronic conditions have a limited effect on mobility. Only 6 percent are confined to the house, 4 percent need help to get around, and 9 percent have some trouble getting around alone. The remaining 81 percent have no limitations of mobility.

IMPLICATIONS FOR THE RECREATOR

This statistical overview contains important implications for recreators working with segments of our elderly population in both private and community recreation facilities. Mature adults are a very diverse group with a wide variety of needs, interests, and problems. Recreation programs must, of necessity, contain flexible scheduling and a wide variety of activities requiring various levels and degrees of active participation if the total needs of this segment of our population are to be met.

SELECTED REFERENCES

Long, L. H., ed. *1971 world almanac.* New York: Newspaper Enterprise Association, 1970.

Metropolitan Life Insurance Co. United Press International, August 3, 1970.

Moss, Sen. Frank E. Health care a right of elderly, Moss says. *Salt Lake Tribune,* May 2, 1975.

United Nations Census Bureau. United Press International, October 4, 1974.

United Nations Report. United Press International, January 18, 1975.

United States Department of Commerce, Bureau of the Census. *Senior citizens— 18 million.* Washington, D.C.: U.S. Government Printing Office, 1964.

United States Department of Health, Education and Welfare. *Aging.* Washington, D.C.: U.S. Government Printing Office, Publication 20, 1955.

United States Department of Health, Education and Welfare. *Aging: Older Americans speak to the nation.* Washington, D.C.: U.S. Government Printing Office, Publication 187, 1970.

United States Department of Health, Education and Welfare. *Working with older people: Biological, psychological, and sociological aspects of aging.* Washington, D.C.: U.S. Government Printing Office, Publication 1459, 1970.

Utah Center for Health Statistics. *Utah public health profile.* Salt Lake City: Utah State Division of Health, 1972.

World Health Organization. United Press International, April 6, 1975.

2
BIOLOGICAL/PHYSIOLOGICAL ASPECTS OF AGING

Youth is a gift of nature. Age is a work of art.
—unknown

Since Ponce de Leon's search for the fountain of youth, humanity has sought methods of prolonging and rejuvenating life. Regretfully, there are no "anti-aging" treatments that are well enough established to warrant general application at the present time and that are without hazardous side effects.

Aging can be described as the sum total of the processes of biological/ physiological, psychological, and sociological changes that occur in an individual from birth throughout the course of life. As time advances, the observable changes or alterations associated with the aging process occur more or less consistently for all mature adults. The chronological age at which these changes become observable can, however, vary greatly from individual to individual. Aging and disease are not considered synonymous. Therefore, the changes associated with aging do not include diagnosable disease states. Although it is possible that the changes attributed to aging may be early signs of specific disease processes, this has yet to be proven.

Although the bodies of knowledge available regarding theories of aging are growing, they are still in formative, hypothetical stages. Because people live under diverse conditions of temperature, diet, sanitation, and other environmental influences and because individuals have diverse genetic makeups, an adequate picture of the fundamental nature of human aging must emerge from clinical findings, family records, and vital statistics. Or inferences can be made based on the results of studies of lower animal forms.

Most of our present knowledge regarding the aging process in humans is based on cross-sectional studies, which are subject to bias from general cultural, economic, environmental, and other conditions that change over time and cannot be controlled. Longitudinal studies could answer many of our questions regarding the aging process in humans. Such studies are not currently available because they are time-consuming, expensive, and extremely difficult to carry out.

The theories about aging and the mechanisms that influence aging can be subdivided according to types of causes into two major groups: intrinsic and extrinsic. These factors decrease the ability of the organism to perform functions that may be necessary to stay alive. Although these intrinsic or extrinsic factors can act independently in their influence on the aging process, a cause-and-effect relationship can also exist, making it possible for one to greatly influence the other.

INTRINSIC FACTORS—THE GENETIC BASIS FOR AGING

Intrinsic factors which influence aging occur inevitably and may be considered as a natural property of the organism, resulting from one or more of the processes and structures characteristic of all living systems. An individual's constitutional inheritance affects the aging process by passing on deficiencies or the predisposition for certain diseases. This inherent genetic makeup determines developmental processes and the time of onset, course and direction, and the time sequence of the various aging processes in the organism. These genetically programmed events occur progressively and inexorably as time progresses in the life of the organism, more or less independently of the environment.

Genes

The genes, which are located on the chromosomes, are the basic determiners of the biological properties of all living beings. There are four basic kinds of genetic effects which might contribute to the aging processes. These include: (1) genes that cause rapid aging or decreased viability and low resistance to disease; (2) genes that, though generally beneficial in early life, slowly produce harmful changes as by-products of normal function; (3) genes for longevity that have not appeared or evolved because they are inconsequential to species reproduction and survival; and (4) genes or gene products that are not accurately reproduced during development, or that are accumulated as a result of so-called somatic mutation.

Evolution

Evolution has given birth to the complexity of all living systems through genetic variation and natural selection. The evolution of a species appears to depend upon the senescence and death of individuals, as provided for in nature. The second law of thermodynamics states that, with time, systems—biological or not—tend to become disordered. If a living system is exposed merely to the passage of time, a number of changes will occur. Most of these changes result in a more disordered arrangement of the molecules and atoms of which the living being is constructed. Such an increase in disorder is referred to as an increase in the entropy of the system. Therefore, it is evident that some deterioration will occur in all living systems, and, in all likelihood, aging is the sum total of these naturally occurring increases in disorder for which evolutionary selection has not produced an effective counteractant.

Molecular Disorders

There are three basic types of molecular disorders which can occur in the human organism during the aging process, in addition to the random formation of new bonds within a molecule. These include: (1) denaturation, or the transformation of a molecule into another shape which no longer possesses biological activity; (2) association, or the accumulation of protein molecules into a weblike matrix which acts as a barrier to free diffusion of other molecules important in the vital function of the cell, thus decreasing the life function of the cell; and (3) cross-linkage, or the formation of linkages between various molecules within cells, which can reduce the maximum work capacity of cells thus affected.

Cell Changes

Cell changes associated with aging are not caused by specific diseases, but by the aging process itself. These cell changes are accompanied by structural changes in the matrix of the tissues, fibers, and fluids through which nutrients are brought to living cells and waste products removed. These changes in the matrix interfere with the nutrition of the cells and cause them to degenerate.

Cellular changes include the loss of certain kinds of organized structures in cells and changes in their architecture or efficiency. The most significant cellular changes include: (1) a reduced capacity for cell growth and tissue repair, including the failure to replace cells as they are destroyed or die off; (2) a gradual drying of tissue; (3) a gradual retardation of the rate of tissue oxidation, or lowering of the speed of living; (4) cellular atrophy, degeneration, increased cell pigmentation, and fatty infiltration; (5) depletion of essential cell or tissue components necessary for the maintenance of normal structure and function, or errors in the function of cellular components; (6) accumulation within cells or tissues of substances which may be chemically or mechanically harmful; (7) a gradual decrease in tissue elasticity and degenerative changes in the elastic connective tissue of the body; (8) a progressive degeneration and atrophy of the nervous system; (9) general impairment of the mechanisms that maintain a fairly constant internal environment for the cells and tissues; and (10) gradual failure of production of a juvenescent or growth substance and an increasing production of an aging factor or hormone.

The nucleus of the cell and the cytoplasm are not immune to the disruptive influences of time and entropy. It has been suggested that, with the passage of time, changes in the genetic code of individual cells occur on a random basis. This is referred to as somatic mutation. A gradual retardation of cell division occurs with age. Moreover, when cells divide, accidental losses or changes in the amount or kind of chromosomal material may occur. Although changes in chromosomes do take place in certain cells during aging, concomitant findings indicate that these changes cannot be the major cause of aging. Thus, the meaning of the chromosomal abnormalities in relationship to aging remains to be explained.

With the passage of time, there occurs within the cells an accumulation of pigmented inclusion bodies in a variety of mammalian tissues, including muscle and nerve cells. This so-called age pigment appears to be an insoluble complex of proteins and lipids that has been altered as a result of reaction with molecular oxygen. Because few observations of structural changes in cells are universally accepted as clear evidence of intrinsic advancing age, these changes can be considered only potential causes of aging. Additional changes in human cell structures can result from changes in nutrition, temperature, endocrine and exocrine secretion, and exposure to the sun. Relationships of these changes to the aging process are uncertain.

Cell Death

Two kinds of cell death occur in aging organisms. The first kind may be called developmental death and occurs in structures such as the skin, blood, and lining of the digestive system as a natural part of the normal functioning of these organs. The production of new cells to take the place of those that have died almost exactly compensates for the old cells. Thus, it is not generally believed at present that developmental or normal cell death is an important causative factor in the aging process. It is quite likely, in fact, that organs and tissues in which a regular replacement of cells takes place do not contribute substantially to the aging process. Rather, aging is primarily a property of those cells and systems in which there is no evolved mechanism for regular replacement, either because such cells are well shielded from the environment, or because they have a long natural lifetime. Indeed, it is probable that cell death is directly related to the degree of its specialization.

Information on cell death or cell loss in nondividing tissues and organs has been established in only a few cell types. It has been shown that the number of large Purkinje cells in the cerebellum, the number of cells in certain spinal ganglia, and the number of axons in certain nerve tracks decrease slowly with age to about 60 to 80 percent of their value in young persons. There is also a decrease in the muscle mass of most aging animals. Whether this is due to a decrease in the size of individual muscle cells or to a loss of numbers of cells has not yet been demonstrated conclusively.

Arrangement of Cells

In addition to the loss of cells that occurs with time, there is also a change in the relative positions of cells. This increased irregularity in the arrangement of cells is one of the few available clues that we have regarding the age of an animal from which a tissue section has been taken. The appearance of the fibrous proteins and the loss of cell elements are other indications. The quantitative measurement of the irregularity of cell arrangement has not yet been undertaken.

During aging, certain changes also take place in the medium surrounding the cells. Space between the individual cells and the blood vessels is occupied by fluids, by various kinds of fibers that bind the tissue together into a coherent mass, and by jellylike coatings on the major surfaces (mucopolysaccharides). Investigation has shown that there is a gradual increase in the amount of insoluble collagen relative to the mucopolysaccharide content of tissues. Even the kinds of mucopolysaccharides change during growth and possible during senescence, but the true physiological meaning of all this is not clear.

Enzymes

We know that loss of cells occurs with age. We also know of age-dependent alterations in the activities of specific enzymes within cells that remain. Available data do not, however, confirm any of the biochemical theories of aging. Nonetheless, selected enzymatic decrements can be offered to explain age-associated declines in some physiological performances. A cell has two general functions: to support the whole organism and to support itself. These functions depend on the cell's ability to produce and utilize energy in synthesizing essential molecules. The governors of synthesis are enzymes. Many reactions occur, each regulated by a specific enzyme. In general, the most striking changes in enzymatic activities occur in early life. Senescence is not accompanied by any uniform change. Thus, it has not been possible to formulate any general hypothesis about the relationship of changes in enzymatic activities to age, even though selected enzymes do show specific age-associated changes.

Hormones

There is a gradual decrease in the amount of certain hormones and the activity of various glandular systems with age. There is a reduced output of anterior pituitary and adrenal cortical hormones, and the hormones from the thyroid and sex glands. Hormone deficiency is not the primary cause of physical aging, though it frequently accelerates and intensifies the process of aging in some organs and organ functions. This is especially true of deficiency of the sex hormones. That the deficiency of the sex hormones is an important factor in physical aging has been demonstrated by the fact that hormonal treatment of aged persons improves their physical strength and vigor. There is, however, a controversy regarding the use of hormonal injections for all aging individuals.

Other

Additional cell-related changes associated with aging include a diminishing of the stretchability of arterial tissue. The stretchable length of fibers diminishes, and the result is a loss of elasticity at high pressure. In addition, cholesterol reduces the amount of elastic fibers in arterial tissue. These alterations reduce the body's capacity to move blood.

The size of cardiac myofibrils and the amount of elastic tissue decrease with aging. Replacement of collagen by elastic tissue also occurs and may interfere with cardiac output.

With aging there is a reduction of muscle mass, and, in certain muscle groups, such as the uterine muscles, connective tissue increases and collagen becomes tougher. Additional changes occur as alterations in neural control and rate of chemical reactions in the human organism and in reductions of blood supply. Inability to maintain high muscular activity in the later years of life may be a reflection of these body changes.

As joints age, the water-absorbing capability of tendons decreases, and collagen fibers aggregate into larger bundles. Both changes cause connective tissue in the joints to stiffen. Changes in the structure of articulating surfaces of joints, attributable to changes in composition of cartilage and its water content, also cause stiffness. Welding together of cartilage surfaces during periods of inactivity adds to stiffness, and lowering of temperature around finger joints accentuates it.

The aging process is accelerated by the accumulation of such substances as iron and calcium in the cytoplasm, the jellylike material of the cell, thus affecting the permeability of the cell material to food and waste products.

Although aging and disease are not synonymous, aging is a biological process which causes increased susceptibility to disease. As tissues become senescent, they provide a favorable environment for some diseases, such as cancer.

EXTRINSIC FACTORS—ENVIRONMENTAL FACTORS THAT MAY CONTRIBUTE TO OR ACCELERATE AGING

Extrinsic factors are environmental influences. They can be modified to some extent and may be of different magnitude in different environments.

Nearly every environmental factor can influence the health, physical condition, and length of life of the human organism. Environment and its potential hazards tend to reduce the probability of human survival as the aging process progresses.

Temperature, Radiation, Chemicals

Temperature affects the rate of aging to about the same extent as it affects metabolic activity. The ability of the human organism to adjust to changes in environmental temperature is reduced with age; thus, the older individual is less effective in meeting the challenges of the environment. Radiation effects of a cumulative and dramatic nature, however, can greatly influence aging. The X rays, cosmic rays, and ultraviolet light to which an individual is exposed may cause mild to severe changes in the body's chemical makeup. Long, continued exposure to ultraviolet light produces injury to the skin, affecting the cells that generate the continually replacing epidermis and causing alteration of the collagen layer underlying the surface layers of the skin and its replacement by elastin. This change in elasticity of the skin results in wrinkling, particularly on the exposed surfaces of the body.

Mechanical Forces

Mechanical forces, or simply the dissipation of physical energy on the organism through bumps, bruises, breaks, abrasions, and other physical trauma or injury caused by mechanical, chemical, and thermal changes, can influence longevity. But, because most of these injuries occur to the outer surface of the body, the reparative process restores the original condition of the organism except for scars. Therefore, such physical injuries are unlikely to be an important contributory factor to the debilities of age except in a small percentage of the population.

Toxic Substances

Toxic substances such as disease in its broadest sense, including bacterial, fungal, animal parasite, and viral infections, can influence longevity. Many of the effects of bacteria are due to the poisonous substances they create and liberate into the bloodstream. These substances may cause changes in the body's cells or tissues far removed from the initial site of the infection. The remarkable increase in lifespan in the past 40 years is, in large measure, due to improvements in hygiene, the development of effective antibiotics to fight disease, and immunization to prevent disease. A current negligence on the part of parents to provide their children with immunization against childhood diseases has caused many school districts to make this immunization a prerequisite for admission into school. Air pollutants, tobacco smoke, and pesticides containing selenium, mercury, lead, and arsenic are classified as additional toxic substances that have the potential to produce pathological changes in the human organism. Humanity, however, can control the use of these substances.

Diet

Diet can shorten or lengthen life. Too much food can shorten life by taxing certain organ systems and fostering specific diseases. A century ago, a large percentage of the U.S. population lived rural lives of hard work and simple diet; today, an ever-increasing percentage of the population is urban, and overeating and lack of exercise frequently are factors in the life-style. In many nations, postwar prosperity was accompanied by a pronounced increase in the fat content of diets and by automation with its resultant lack of exercise. This apparently has caused an increase in susceptibility to many degenerative, age-associated pathologies, particularly arteriosclerosis, which is reflected in the high incidence of heart disease and cerebral vascular accidents in mature adults. Insurance statistics clearly indicate a strong inverse correlation between overweight, even to a mild degree, and life span. Omission from the diet of essential nutrients such as a vitamin or an essential amino acid can result in the malfunction of body cells, thus shortening life. Chronic or periodic undernutrition may be an important cause of aging in populations in certain areas of the world, as indicated by vital statistics.

Social Milieu

Our social milieu, our contemporary life-style, and the adverse influences of, or interaction with, other human beings may influence longevity. Habits that the individual acquires from parents in such matters as cleanliness, rest, and general psychological outlook play an extremely important role in the ability to preserve physical integrity as one ages. This includes the influence of alcohol, tobacco, and drugs in a person's life. The use of alcohol in moderate quantities does not seem to appreciably affect longevity; in fact, moderate users as a group have a better life expectancy than the total abstainers. Extreme alcoholism, however, leads to many deteriorative changes: the liver, for example, may become hardened through the double processes of cell loss and replacement of normal cells by collagenous connective tissue. Although heredity helps to determine an individual's ability to adjust or adapt to life's stresses, psychological or sociological events that cause worry, fatigue, and constant muscular tension, coupled with improper physical activity, may constitute a life-style or personal emotional makeup that would tend to exhaust genetic energies and result in premature aging.

SUMMARY—INTRINSIC AND EXTRINSIC FACTORS

It is difficult to interpret the known data concerning the biology of aging because individuals with diverse genetic constitutions are likely to respond differently to various environmental conditions according to their own particular genetic makeup. In addition, it is quite unlikely that a single factor or process may be underlying all of aging from birth to old age. It is probable that a number of factors—some building up or maintaining the organism, some tearing it down—may be operating, to a greater or lesser extent, at different times in an individual's life to achieve that person's particular pattern of aging and, ultimately, death in old age.

Humans have the ability to retard, but not to abolish, the effects of time and environment on longevity. The effects of various disruptive environmental factors have already been reduced by public health measures, information on diets, and promotion of safety practices. Better diet and hygiene, combined with the prevention and treatment of new growth and degenerative diseases, and improved organ and tissue transplantation may continue to increase longevity. But senescence and, finally, death from old age are the result of the interaction between inherited factors for survival and adverse environmental factors and are ultimate and inescapable consequences of human biology.

EXTERNAL SIGNS OF AGING

An aged human being can usually be recognized by the appearance of the individual's skin and hair, speed of movement, gait, posture, and the degree of loss of vigor and vitality.

The face tells the individual's age more forcibly than any other part of the body, especially the lower part of the face. Due to loss of teeth or wearing down of the teeth, the jaw becomes smaller and the chin sags. The cheeks become pendulous, with wrinkles and bags, and the eyelids become baggy with the upper lids overhanging the lower. The eyes seem dull and lusterless, and they often have a watery look due to the poor functioning of the tear glands. The nose elongates in vertical dimension. As the lower part of the face is shortened by changes in the jaw, the nose appears to be larger than it actually is.

Most elderly people have lost some or all of their teeth. The culprit in tooth loss at later ages is gum disease, the result of tartar deposits below the gum level. Tooth loss governs how well we chew, which in turn affects nutrition. Even with the best dentures, tooth loss is likely to change the shape of the mouth and the facial expression. Under the dentures, atrophic changes take place in the bones, and the dentures become loose and act as irritants. This often causes speech problems, especially lisping.

Changes in the facial skin, as well as the skin covering the entire body, are very marked. The epidermis gradually thins and becomes more flexible, rubbery, and flaccid with age. Under the epidermis, the tissues are less elastic than they formerly were because of atrophy of many of the elastic fibers that make up a considerable share of the intercellular matrix. Because of loss of elasticity, the skin springs back less readily, it sags here and there, and creases or folds are fixed as wrinkles.

Atrophy of the oil and sweat glands makes the skin rather dry and coarse. Perspiration is less profuse, even in areas of the body where formerly it was abundant. In true senility, dark spots or white scaly plaques often appear in exposed areas of the skin. Moles, warts, and other skin blemishes often appear as age advances.

The hair on the head becomes thin and gray. Gradually it becomes so thin that the head is bald or nearly bald, especially in the case of men. The gray color turns into white, often with a yellowish cast. Tough, bristly hairs grow around the openings of the external ears and the nose. The hairs of the eyebrows usually become coarse and more bristly, though they may not change in color as the hair on the head changes.

The nails of the hands and feet become thick and tough, with a slight increase in brittleness. The hands show the ravages of age, not only by the toughened, rough skin that characteristically develops at this time, but also by the veins that show clearly on the backs of the hands.

The arms and legs are likely to be flabby and unattractive, with veins showing through in the legs. The feet frequently grow larger because of sagging muscles, and they develop corns, bunions, and other disfigurations which necessitate the wearing of larger and less attractive shoes.

The individual's stature decreases, and there is a stooping of the shoulders, thus making the individual appear smaller. Because of poor eating habits, stemming from food dislikes, difficulties in eating, or economic factors, many elderly men and women are approximately 10 percent above their desirable weight. Others lose weight with advancing years as a result of poor health or poor eating habits.

There is a gradual shrinking of the secondary sex characteristics with advancing age, and the body does not seem to be either masculine or feminine. Loss of muscular tone and stiffness of the joints cause difficulties in locomotion. The gait of the aged shows a shortened step, lack of elasticity, a widened base, and a forward leaning in a slightly fixed attitude.

Tremors of the hands, forearms, head, and lower jaw are common among old people, although the tremors are not necessarily continuously present. They are usually increased by fatigue, emotions, or activity in the part of the body involved. Restless movements, such as tapping, twitching, patting, or rocking the body, may be common.

INTERNAL SIGNS OF AGING—PHYSIOLOGICAL CHANGES

External signs of aging are the reflection of a number of internal or physiological changes in structure, chemical makeup, and functional effectiveness of various organs of the body and their component parts. These internal or physiological changes are not as readily observable as external changes but are as pronounced and widespread.

Patterns of age differences may appear in the human organism in various physiological characteristics, some of which are maintained into advanced age, while others peak in middle life and then decrease. The most common pattern, however, is a gradual decline that begins in adulthood and continues throughout life. There are known structural changes that underlie the gross functional failures associated with the aging process. Many physiological characteristics remain constant in resting conditions but, with advancing age, show significant differences when the human organism is placed in stressful situations.

Vital Capacity Changes

Changes in pulse rate and oxygen consumption are more varied, respiratory minute volume is more pronounced, and resumption of normal respiration following exercise is much slower in older than in younger persons. With increased age there is a small, but significant, decrease in average residual lung volume and a somewhat less effective gas exchange in the lungs. This is caused by the fact that the lungs gradually become inelastic, smaller, and, in general, less viable. Chest excursion may be hampered by the rigidity of the thorax because of the calcification of cartilaginous tissue. An inability to inhale or expand the chest fully results in a substantial reduction in maximum breathing capacity and vital capacity. These changes result in a decrease in vital lung capacity and the ability of the human organism to use oxygen.

Central Nervous System Changes

The cells of the central nervous system are incapable of self-duplication. With age there is a gradual reduction in the number of cells in the central nervous system, and some changes occur within those cells that do survive. Microscopic studies show degeneration of nerve ganglion cells and the highly specialized supporting elements of the nervous system. Changes in the nervous system are especially marked in the brain. In old age there is a gradual loss in brain weight and size; the lateral ventricles tend to be dilated, and the ribbon of cortical tissue is narrowed. Central nervous system changes come early in the aging period, as is shown by a decrease first in the speed and later in the power of intelligence. Anderson and Langton (1970) indicate that, with brain atrophy and cellular degeneration, there occurs increased cerebrospinal fluid, thickened dura mater, and a decrease of general blood circulation with a resultant decrease in metabolism. Such alterations are manifested in a slower learning and motor response, visual inability to accommodate near points (presbyopia), and a decrease in auditory acuity.

In 1975 Dr. David Drachman, Northwestern University neurologist, found a highway of nerve endings that could control a major aging process in the brain. His research indicates that specific nerve highways, rather than brain secretions, may control thinking and memory, and the possible repair of highways damaged by old age through strokes and other vessel diseases or loss of function in some neurons may eventually be possible.

Musculoskeletal Changes

With senescence come a number of musculoskeletal changes. Cartilage loses water and calcification or hardening of the bones occurs, causing joints to fuse at the cartilage surface. Articular degeneration and, eventually, arthritis occurs at the joints. A softening of bony structures is the result of absorption of mineral matter. Metabolic by-products, such as mineral salts, accumulate with age and may help to modify the internal structures of the bones by promoting cross-linkages, especially in the connective-tissue collagen. Such structural changes in the skeletal system underlie stiffness and inflexibility of joints and increase bone fragility. Such brittle bones are subject to fractures and breaks that become increasingly slow in healing as age progresses. Bone fragility has been found to be more intimately related to endocrine changes, decreased use or inactivity, and loss of muscle tone than to the level of the individual's nutrition.

Although striated muscle is said to lose mass with age, little is known about the intracellular changes that take place in aging muscles. Lowered muscular strength usually results from a gradual loss in the cellular elements in the muscles, thus causing a degeneration and atrophy of muscle fibers. Decreased activity or disuse can also accentuate osteoporoses and muscular atrophy, all of which result in strength loss. Motor efficiency, including speed, strength, endurance, coordination, and flexibility diminish very slowly during the mature adult period and increase in rate of decline after the fifth decade. How much this decline is dependent upon the aging process and how much upon decreased muscular activity is not clearly established. It has been demonstrated, in many cases, that those who continue to participate extensively in physical activities lose their motor abilities at a much slower rate than those who do not. Some of the physical degeneration that occurs in the aging process can be duplicated in the young by enforced inactivity. Such enforced inactivity produces a decrease in muscle size, strength, endurance, power, coordination, flexibility, a deterioration of bone cells, and the development of poor digestion.

Motor Capacity Changes

The musculoskeletal changes associated with aging (physical changes and psychological factors) result in changes in motor capacity, primarily because of the accompanying decrease in strength and energy. Emotional tensions may hasten these changes in motor capacity or decrease the individual's motivation to perform at maximum efficiency. Regardless of the extenuating circumstances, few individuals can hope to keep their motor abilities up to the peak performance achieved during youth. Motor capacity changes, like other age-associated changes, are not consistent within or between individuals. However, the changes in strength, speed, and skill are the most important changes in regard to personal and social adjustment.

Strength

Strength and work capacity diminish very slowly as the ability to use muscles declines, primarily because of muscular flabbiness and general weakness. The ability for brief and violent effort diminishes with age, while the ability to withstand a long, steady grind increases. Physical fatigue requires longer time for recuperation with advancing age. This is also true of fatigue from continual mental work or from nervous strain. As a result, most old people learn to cut down on any work that requires either strength or speed.

Decline in physical strength begins in the mid-twenties and advances throughout the adult years. All strength tests verify this loss. In an average grip-strength test at age 60, hand strength has been found to have declined by 17 percent from the maximum exhibited in youth. By 75 years, the maximum grip-strength is approximately equal to that of 12- to 15-year-olds (Shock 1962). Decline in strength with age varies, however, with different groups of muscles. The decline is most pronounced in the flexor muscles of the forearm and in the muscles that raise the body. Declining strength is shown also in the speed with which the elderly person becomes fatigued, even after only short periods of activity.

Speed

Speed is an attribute of youth. Tests of both simple and complex reaction time indicate that elderly subjects are significantly slower than younger subjects and they become increasingly slower as the difficulty of the task is increased (Birren 1963). Decline occurs slowly from 12 years of age on and then speeds up abruptly after 60. In addition, older subjects require more time to organize a response or to develop a state of expectancy than do younger subjects. Fatigue, stress, tension, and other factors affect the velocity of reaction time, thus increasing individual differences in this aspect of aging.

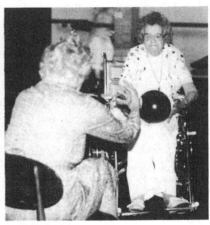

Skill

Skilled movements, learned earlier in life, tend to become slower with advanced age. This slowness may be influenced by the decreased frequency of use of specific skills. Tests involving simple manual skills clearly verify a decline in speed of performance with age (Talland 1962). Slowing down in industry by aged persons is commonly reported even though many workers try to keep their production up to previous standards by increased conscientiousness (Chown and Heron 1965).

Because motor coordinations become increasingly difficult with advancing age, there is a tendency for old people to become awkward and clumsy in their movements, which causes them to spill and drop things, to trip and fall, and to do things in a careless, untidy manner. The breakdown of motor skills proceeds in inverse order to that in which the skills were formed: the earliest formed skills are retained longest, and the most recently formed ones are lost first. With advancing age, however, even the most firmly established coordinations begin to break up, and the individual reverts to the state of semihelplessness characteristic of the early part of life.

The tendency to be awkward, together with the greater amount of energy needed to do things than was formerly necessary, very often causes older people to shun motor activities whenever possible. As a result of voluntarily giving up activities, often before it is necessary, many old people are more in danger of wearing out from disuse than from sensible activity. Continued exercise of a skill, on the other hand, can delay the decline of that skill.

Learning new skills in old age is an unusual experience. Not only is learning more difficult than it formerly was, but lack of motivation on the individual's part further militates against learning. When learning skills that will be of personal benefit, the individual will gain sufficient motivation to put forth the necessary effort, though the learning will progress more slowly, and the end results will be inferior to those of younger learners (Entwisle 1959).

The role of motivation in learning new skills is well documented. Measures of steadiness in the hand and arm have shown that many 70-year-olds are as steady or even steadier than younger people. This suggests that older individuals are capable of learning new skills and of doing good skilled work if they have the necessary motivation and the needed opportunities.

Exercise and Aging

According to Mateeff (1964), exercise and its associated tissue stimulation is the vital factor that alone is capable of not only stopping the processes of involution and atrophy but also of reversing them, thus promoting and bringing into play the processes of self-repair and self-renovation at the molecular level in organisms of the aging. Planned and progressive exercise can produce such positive gains as increased strength and skeletal muscle hypertrophy, hypertrophy of the heart with resultant training effect of a decreased heart rate, increased ability to expend energy, more efficient use of oxygen, a greater vital capacity, and improved body suppleness from increased joint mobility. Bortz (1963) indicated that physical activity helps to delay the diminution of sex-hormone excretion. Activity can maintain the anabolic protein-building qualities of the sex glands and concomitant muscle strength. Physically active older persons, as a group, express a higher level of vitality, ability to sleep, mental capacity, and desire for socialization than their sedentary counterparts.

Cellular System Changes

There is a gradual reduction in the performance of many organ systems with advanced age. This may be due to a gradual loss of functional units (gradual loss of cells because cell division or replacement diminishes with age), to a gradual impairment in the remaining cell units, or to a combination of both. Universal observations verify the accumulation of specific (lipofuscin) pigments in nerve cells, liver cells, myocardium cells, and other cells in the aging body. The general phenomenon of cell dysfunction is related to age changes in a variety of cellular processes. Most cellular systems show a linear decrement that begins in the forties and continues throughout life; i.e., because of the gradual loss of cellular elements in the brain and nerves, speed of conduction of the nerve impulses decreases with age (Wolff 1959).

Tissue Changes

Degenerative, age-dependent diseases such as ateriosclerosis involve structural changes in the human organism. Research findings indicate that, with aging, there is an increase in connective tissue in the body and a subsequent and gradual loss of elasticity in this tissue (Hurlock 1968). The loss of elasticity of human skin during aging appears to reflect deterioration of collagen fibers in the underlying supportive tissues of the skin. This deterioration gives the skin a wrinkled and flaccid appearance. A similar loss in elasticity of large human arteries has been related to the change in characteristics of collagen and calcification of the elastin in the arterial wall. Collagenous substances within the connective tissues of the body, such as those found in tendons and ligaments, become hardened and inelastic with age.

Such tissue change also occurs in the various organs of the human organism. Perhaps the most marked change is to be found in the cardiovascular system. Aging affects the cardiovascular system's efficiency and subsequently results in alterations in the rate and efficiency of oxygen-nutrient utilization. Marked changes take place in the heart. In the early years of life, the position of the heart is more nearly in the center of the chest than it is in advanced age. Also, its position is more erect in the young individual while later, in middle and old age, it assumes a more horizontal position. It increases in bulk—connective tissue and fat content within inner-surface membranes and cavities—with age and continues to grow even after the body has ceased to do so. Therefore, the ratio of heart weight to body weight increases gradually with age. The softness and pliability of the valves gradually change because of an increase in fibrous tissue from deposits of fat and calcium, and from changes in the quality of the elastic tissue. Valves become inelastic, resulting in a tendency toward dilation and muscular incompetency in the heart, with subsequent arrhythmia.

The coronary arteries supplying the heart become thickened at their inner-most lining (intima). Blood vessels, particularly arteries, display age by their inelasticity and thinning muscular walls. Stretched arteries become more twisted in their course. Degeneration and the collecting of fat deposits further weaken artery walls. Structural arterial change is followed by a functional rise in systolic blood pressure and a lowering of diastolic pressure.

Blood Changes

Many biochemical characteristics of the blood are well maintained within normal ranges, even into advanced years. If, however, the older human organism is placed in a stressful environment, which causes an increase in the acid, alkali, or glucose level of the blood, a longer period of time is necessary for the body to bring these blood levels back to normal. Thus, alterations in the sugar content and acidity of the blood are overcome more slowly and less completely with advancing age. In addition, as the human organism ages, its capacity to produce immune bodies slowly diminishes.

Both cross-sectional and longitudinal research (Hurlock 1968) tend to indicate that the blood cholesterol continues to rise until about ages 55 to 60 years and then falls substantially. This blood condition can be considered an actual improvement of physiologic status after age 60.

Up to approximately age 70, there is a progressive increase in the peripheral resistance to blood flow by the blood vessels in many vascular beds. This is accompanied by a progressive rise or elevation in average blood-pressure valves due to the increased rigidity of the walls of the aorta and central arteries, a decrease in renal blood flow (ascribed to a gradual loss of functioning nephrons), blood filtration rate, and cardiac output. This increase in resistance requires more work by the heart to maintain the same flow of blood.

Internal Secretion Changes

There is a decrease in the concentration of hormone and endocrine excre-tions with advancing age, resulting in a very gradual decline of the bodily functions controlled by these various excretions. Of primary importance are the decreases in endocrine gland secretions that result in a decreased resistance to infection and the decreases in androgenic hormones that cause increased muscle-tissue atrophy.

Excretion of sex hormones, and the reproductive organs themselves, decline rapidly and cease to function at about 50 years of age for the female and 65 years for the male. See Sexual Changes (pp. 28-29) for a more detailed description of these changes.

Digestive Changes

Digestive changes are perhaps the most marked of the regulatory functions. Difficulties in eating, which usually result from loss of teeth, are accompanied by a decline in smell and taste sensitivity, causing even the best food to be somewhat tasteless.

As a general rule, old people eat less primarily because they do not feel the need or desire for food. When they do eat, it is usually in smaller quantities and at more frequent intervals. Old people cannot tolerate long periods of starvation because their blood sugar falls to undesirably low levels.

Frequently, older individuals need more fluids to lubricate and dissolve food elements. The lower bowel, or colon, is more sensitive to irritation by roughage because it is less well lubricated with mucus. This is especially serious for old people whose loss of teeth makes it difficult for them to chew food properly. Colitis can be a common digestive problem resulting from changes in the functional efficiency of the digestive system.

Changes in Sleep

The amount and quality of sleep needed by the human organism declines with age. By the age of 60 or 70 years, the daily amount of sleep is reduced an hour or two, and brief periods of rest and sleep, "cat naps," generally replace the longer periods of sleep of the younger person. Many old people suffer from insomnia and an increase in disturbed sleep. These changes in sleep patterns can contribute to daytime tiredness, which appears to increase markedly after the age of 65 years.

Body Temperature Changes

Because of the decreased vascularity of their skin, old people cannot tolerate extremes of temperature, either hot or cold. Reduced metabolic rate and lessened muscular vigor make regulation of body temperature difficult in cold environments, and the degeneration of the capillaries and sweat glands in the skin make regulation of body temperature difficult in hot environments. As a group, however, old people feel the cold more than the heat.

Sensory Changes

The function of all of the various sense organs decreases in efficiency as age advances. Frequently this decline in efficiency of use is slow and gradual, providing the individual an opportunity to make adequate adjustments. In addition, modern aids in the form of glasses for impaired vision and hearing aids for impaired hearing compensate for the decline to such an extent that the adjustments can be almost perfect.

The most useful of all the sense organs, the eyes and ears, are the most seriously affected by old age. The marked decrease in the efficiency of the eyes may be caused by poor care during the years of maturity, a generally lowered physical condition, and significant decrease in pupil size associated with the aging process. Difficulties in near vision and color vision are common in old age.

Deterioration in hearing is greatest for high-pitched sounds. Many old people regard hearing difficulties as caused by the stimulus rather than the response. They blame others for mumbling and do not recognize the fact that the trouble may lie within themselves. In personal conversations with just one person, the hearing-impaired elderly usually have little difficulty because they can face the speaker directly and read lips. In groups, on the other hand, the old person with a severe hearing loss must be close to and directly facing the speaker in order to hear what is being said.

Changes in taste are marked in old age and are caused by atrophy of the taste buds, with those at the end of the tongue atrophying first. In addition, taste buds become fewer on the inner surface of the cheeks. The sense of smell becomes less acute with age and tends to make food seem tasteless.

With the drying and hardening of the skin, the sense of touch becomes less and less acute, and sensitivity to pain declines. These declines begin after the age of 45 and become more marked after 60.

Diminution of sensory experiences removes the elderly from many sources of enjoyment. No longer, for example, is eating as pleasurable as it formerly was, nor can the individual enjoy visual and auditory sensations to the same extent because of poor vision or poor hearing. Declining sensitivity is likely to result in social isolation, especially when the sense organs that are most seriously affected are the eyes and ears. And, finally, personality maladjustments are frequent among old people when the use of their senses has declined to the point where they are cut off from social contacts and must live within themselves. This, therefore, can be one of the major adjustment problems associated with physical decline.

Sexual Changes

Although both sexes experience a climacteric, or termination of reproductive capacity, with advancing age, the time of onset and duration are quite different for each sex.

The female climacteric, menopause, or cessation of menstrual periods, usually takes place around age 45. Wide variation does exist, however, in the time of onset. This variation is influenced by heredity, general health, and variations in climate and is caused by ovarian failure or hypoovarianism. Menopause, accompanied by disequilibrium in the endocrine interactional system, causes physical and emotional symptoms in the female. The average length of the climacteric period in the female is two years. Frequently, endocrine treatment in the form of estrogen is used to slow down the speed of the internal changes associated with the menopause. It is a well-established fact that hormones and other properly selected medications are effective and safe during this time and do not prolong the period of menopause. Estrogen replacement therapy should only be used, however, under direct supervision of a physician. The common symptoms, with physiological causes, that accompany menopause are flushes involving the head, neck, and upper thorax, sweats, and hot flashes or tingling that involve the entire body. Parker (1961) says,

Menopause is a transition period, not a climax. It signifies only one thing, a release from the responsibilities of fertility. It is not the end of being a mature woman, with all the term signifies. It is not the beginning of old age or senility.

In comparison to the rapid rate in females, the male climacteric begins at a very slow rate in the 60s or 70s and is accompanied by a very gradual weakening in the male sexual and reproductive powers. Because the process is very slow in the human male, his need for adjustment is not as pronounced. A decline in gonadal functioning is responsible for the changes that accompany the male climacteric. This frequently is accompanied by a decrease in sexual potency and often of libido or sexual desire. It is usual for benign prostatic hypertrophy to accompany this decline in sexual potency in the human male. Like women, many men experience hot flushes, fits of perspiration, chill sensations, especially cold feet, numbness in their hands and feet, and tingling sensations.

In both sexes, the climacteric period is accompanied by a waning of the secondary sex characteristics and a tendency to put on weight. Because of these changes, this period is frequently described as the "third sex" or "neuter gender."

This decline in sexual potency in both sexes is not necessarily accompanied by a decline in sexual desire or the ability to have intercourse. The strength or weakness of the sex drive after the climacteric period will depend on the general health of the individual as well as the type of sexual adjustments made earlier in life. Individuals who made poor sexual adjustments earlier in life usually lose their sex drive earlier than those who made better sexual adjustments when they were younger.

Individual Differences

Older individuals are a very diverse group. These differences are the result of different hereditary endowments, socioeconomic and educational backgrounds, and patterns of living. In addition, aging takes place at different rates for the two sexes. Differences in social, cultural, and economic experiences, extending over a long period of time, tend to increase with age, meaning that the older the group, the more diverse the group. Parker (1961) says,

> It is obvious that some individuals are physically old at 40 and some young at 60 as measured by their physical abilities and activity. And that at 75 one individual is young and spry, while another is old and decrepit. Individuals have different rates of aging that do not correspond to the years they have lived.

The biological or physiological age of the heart, kidney, lungs, even the nerves of one individual of age 60 may differ as much as 50 percent from the same tissue or organ in another person of the same age. In addition, with advancing age an individual's reaction to environmental situations changes. Havinghurst (1965) says,

> From middle age onward, the person confronts changes in the social environment and in his physical body which require readjustments on his part. Society does things to him, and his body changes negatively, but different personalities react differently to the same set of societal pressures and the same set of bodily changes.

In addition to aging differences between individuals, considerable variability also exists within each individual. The life spans of the different organs or systems within the human organism are varied. The ovaries, for example, function for a predictable number of years and then become dormant. Disease may hasten the menopause just as accident or disease may hasten the loss of elasticity in the lenses of the eyes. Normally, however, the life span of the different organs is determined by some "peculiar and obscure physiological time clock inherent within some particular genes of the hereditary constitution" (Hurlock 1968). Thus, an individual's kidneys may be functioning as inefficiently as those of an 80-year-old, the heart may be functioning as well as a 60-year-old, and the chronological age may be 70.

These wide individual differences among organ systems represent the source of many of the medical and sociological problems of older persons. Because aged individuals vary so greatly in total physiological capacity, they are less homogenous than other age groups and must be assessed and dealt with by the recreation specialist and other professionals as individuals rather than as members of a specific age group.

SELECTED REFERENCES

Anderson, C., and Langton. Senile dementia. *Radiology*, 1970, *116*, 85.

Birren, J. E. Research on the psychological aspects of aging. *Geriatrics*, 1963, *18*, 393-403.

Bortz, E. L. *Creative aging*. New York: Macmillan, 1963.

Chown, S. M., and Heron, A. Psychological aspects of aging in man. *Annual Review of Psychology*, 1965, *16*, 417-450.

Drachman, David A. No fountain of youth in sight but mind-aging hopes rise. United Press International, June 2, 1975.

Entwisle, D. G. Aging: the effects of previous skills on training. *Occupational Psychology*, 1959, *33*, 238-243.

Havinghurst, R. J. Body, self and society. *Social Sociology Research*, 1965, *49*, 261-267.

Hurlock, Elizabeth B. *Developmental psychology*. 3rd ed. New York: McGraw-Hill, 1968.

Mateeff, D. Problems of the fight for longevity. *Quest*, Monograph III, December 1964, Tucson, Ariz.

Parker, E. *The seven ages of woman*. Baltimore: Johns Hopkins, 1961.

Shock, N. W. The physiology of aging. *Scientific American*, 1962, *206*, no. 1, 100-110.

Talland, G. A. The effect of age on speed of simple manual skill. *Journal of Genetic Psychology*, 1962, *100*, 69-76.

United States Department of Health, Education and Welfare. *Working with older people: Biological, psychological, and sociological aspects of aging*. Washington, D.C.: U.S. Government Printing Office, Publication 1459, 1970.

Wolff, K. *The biological, sociological, and psychological aspects of aging*. Springfield, Ill.: Charles C. Thomas, 1959.

3
PSYCHOLOGICAL ASPECTS OF AGING

As it is not every wine, so it is not every disposition
that grows sour with age.

—Cicero

Psychological age refers to the individual's capacity to adapt to the constantly changing environment. This is classified by many psychologists as the 50-plus years following the attainment of legal age and includes such things as sensory functions, perception, memory and learning, thinking and problem solving, motor skills, motivation, attitudes, personality, and factors of mood and morale to sustain adaptation and productivity. Motivation and adjustment, in addition to the individual's perception of what constitutes a worthwhile role, are critical aspects of psychological aging.

The psychological aspects of aging do not necessarily parallel the biological/physiological aspects of aging. In fact, they usually occur later in life and follow a less uniform developmental sequence. Parker (1961) says,

> *Psychological aging is not to be measured in terms of capabilities alone,*
> *but in the use to which they have been applied from early age through*
> *all the years of maturity. This consists of a blending of a desire to learn,*
> *the ability to wonder and to derive satisfaction and pleasure there-from,*
> *a diversity of interests, and the will to make the necessary effort.*

Adult life is a process of continual change as the individual is faced with new tasks that require adaptation to new circumstances, each of which is associated with a particular amount of "role uncertainty." Role change and the uncertainties that accompany such change are important in all stages of life. They include such things as courtship, marriage, childbirth, career changes,

changes of residence, retirement, death of peers or spouse, and changes in appearance, body function, and health.

Throughout the adult life span, the individual's capacities to solve problems and adapt will be challenged by situations that may be novel to that person although they are characteristic of a particular age level or group. For the mature adult, adequate adaptation to earlier life problems, in addition to present adaptive capacities, increases the likelihood that the individual will be able to cope with and resolve the tasks unique to later life. If, however, the older individual's capacity for adaptation diminishes, even a task characteristic of that person's specific age level may precipitate a crisis or an emotional problem.

We are in a current state of rapid social change and there are no set standards to help individuals adjust to many twentieth-century social roles. For example, social changes have brought about the trend toward early marriage, thus altering the social roles and models in our society for preretirement living, which results in uncertainties for many individuals regarding their role in family life. When their children are grown, women frequently seek employment outside of the home, which can create new psychological issues, especially if the husband's career has become stable and boring. Such happenings can be mid life turning points for marriages.

Despite great social change, adult life maintains a characteristic rhythm. There are certain basic concerns and moods associated with characteristic episodes of the adult life span. Middle-aged persons as a group show more sensitivity to problems of health in themselves and in friends. They tend to attach great importance to the immediate physical environment, and their general reluctant attitude toward a household move contrasts with the easy residential mobility of the younger adult. An event such as changing the place of residence can be a very traumatic experience and an actual turning point in the psychological and social life of the older individual, which may precipitate health problems or exacerbate previously existing health conditions.

FACTORS INFLUENCING PSYCHOLOGICAL ADJUSTMENT

An individual's psychological and sociological environments can influence the length as well as the quality of his or her life. This would include such important considerations as sanitation, preventive health care, and accident prevention. When and if these psychological and sociological factors become relatively stable for all members of society, differences in genetic backgrounds will probably become more important and eventually dominate longevity and aging.

General Health

Most old people are not in poor health. Poor health, therefore, is not a part of growing old because it can be prevented by diet, exercise, and good living habits. Statistics indicate that, although 75 percent of the population over age 65 do have some chronic condition of poor health, only 6 percent are housebound and only 13 percent have a major limitation of their activity.

Research tends to indicate that poor health weakens the morale of individuals in low socioeconomic groups more than that of persons in high socioeconomic groups. Persons in low economic groups struggle for simple subsistence. The consequences of their problems of ill health are magnified by the combination of disease, low economic status, and social isolation. In contrast, higher economic groups are more achievement-oriented. They tend to seek professional services and have higher personal standards and expectations. It has also been found that regional differences can influence the health and behavioral capacities of populations. But socioeconomic influences are greater factors than variations in climate.

Central Nervous System

It is speculated that the central nervous system reflects disease, aging, and vulnerability to disease and other stresses and that it is the pacemaker or central indicator in the process of aging. The central nervous system is the pathway by which environmental factors have health consequences on the human organism primarily because this system is shaped by the unique experiences of the individual and because the cells of this system are critical in influencing bodily functions. Because neurons don't die, they serve to integrate the various functions of the body and can spread the effects of their own age change to other organ systems and remote tissue in the body. Therefore, the biological changes of the nervous system can be said to underlie deterioration of behavioral capacities and health. (See Biological/ Physiological Aspects of Aging, chapter 2.)

Evidence also suggests that the central nervous system's response to important restrictions and other changes in the activity patterns of the individual will produce a chain of crises. Serious, if not terminal, illnesses may be precipitated. For instance, the aging individual, whose loss of coordination leads to recurrent falls, may surrender his or her roles in community activities, stay home, become depressed, lose appetite, and become vulnerable to infection.

Sensory Systems

Sensory-system impairments can be the result of age-related diseases, occupational injuries, or age-related changes in the receptors. Most sensory receptors do become less sharp, slow down, and require more energy to reach a threshold level of stimulation with advancing age. Statistics indicate that 1 out of every 4 persons between the ages of 60 and 80 (250 per 1000 population) has a significant hearing impairment and 1 out of every 12½ persons in this age group (80 per 1000 population) are blind. It is necessary, therefore, for many individuals over age 60 to adapt to some type of sensory change that reduces the amount of information received from the environment. This, quite obviously, reduces the information on which individuals with impaired senses base their behavior. (See Biological/Physiological Aspects of Aging, chapter 2.)

The sensory changes associated with advancing age effectively reduce alertness. Many elderly individuals, as a consequence of reduced sensory input, must become more conscious of behavior to monitor and recheck sensory input before making some movements, such as judging automobiles and traffic lights before crossing the street. Evidence also suggests that some older persons must monitor their own body movements visually to secure proper placement. Therefore, because previously automatic movements of walking or eating need to be watched, the aged reduce their attention to the environment. Compensations for sensory losses are achieved in part through closer monitoring, increased intensity of stimuli, and slowness and cautiousness. For a small proportion of older individuals, compensating for sensory fading is difficult. Raising the level of sensory stimulation, such as intensity of sound or brightness of light, will not automatically result in increased sensory input or perception. Hearing aids, for example, can raise the sound level of incoming signals, but do not necessarily result in improved speech perception. The focal issue is the capacity or resolving power of the central nervous system to handle the information received from the sensory system. Older individuals often, therefore, have to be evaluated with regard to sensory acuity and central resolving power, placing emphasis on changes in peripheral sensory structures and the central integrating role of the nervous system.

There is not, therefore, always a direct relationship between sensory acuity and effective behavior in the aged. Old adults, however, will tend to adapt to their sensory limitations and avoid stress situations. Many older drivers, for example, avoid night driving because of relative insensitivity to light and susceptibility to the effects of glare. The aging individual requires more time to respond to stimuli for two reasons: he requires more time to receive the same amount of information from his environment, and he is more cautious because he knows errors subject him to increased risk. Older individuals, therefore, want and need more sensory information from the environment before responding to stimuli.

Motor Performance

With advancing age many motor skills may cease to have the automatic quality that existed earlier in life. Conditioned reflexes are usually slower in older individuals. Motor skills involve a complex chain reaction of events integrated by the central nervous system and continuous excitation and inhibition of neural activity if the resulting muscle movements are to comprise a graded distribution of sequential activity. If there are delays or reductions in sensory information about a limb position or the contracted state of a muscle, smoothness or speed of the voluntary activity is disrupted. (See Biological/Physiological Aspects of Aging, chapter 2.)

Changes in motor skills in persons over age 65 may contribute to their high accident rate; statistics do indicate that accidents are the sixth largest cause of death, with falls at the top of the list. There is, however, a high relationship between low levels of physical fitness and repeated falls. Therefore, properly prescribed physical activity to help attain and maintain high levels of fitness in individuals over age 65 is an excellent preventive measure that should be stressed in all recreation programs. In the new generation of older persons now emerging, early-life strenuous activities such as tennis, long-distance swimming and running, alpine and nordic skiing, snowshoeing, and other heavy sports persist as fun, thus opening many recreational outlets for this new group of senior citizens.

Work vs. Retirement

Retirement may be a crushing blow to the individual, especially if the person has many years of productivity ahead and wants to work. It can also mean free time, and its use in meaningful ways can involve a major crisis of personal values and reorientation. Because income brings with it a sense of power and accomplishment, a declining self-image frequently accompanies retirement. If income is adequate, the retirement adjustment period for most individuals is two years. If income is severely reduced at retirement, it may cause such a blow to the individual's ego and pocketbook that a somatic illness could develop and set the stage for mental problems or expose hidden personality difficulties. (See Sociological Aspects of Aging, chapter 4.)

Although individuals, especially scientists, are said to hit their stride in creativity and productivity around age 30 to 40 (the peak of creativity follows closely the period of intense intellectual growing occurring in college and graduate school), many individuals continue to make significant scholarly contributions, especially in literature and art, beyond age 70. Length of career preparation is, however, a critical factor. Martha Graham at the age of 83 is still teaching dance and doing choreography; Michaelangelo was the chief architect of St. Peter's Basilica until his death at the age of 89; Toscanini was still conducting his orchestra at the age of 87; and Tennyson and Victor Hugo did important writing in their 80s.

An important factor in these individuals' productivity late in life can be attributed to their emotional state and social productivity. Human beings need to feel useful and productive. If they do not, their emotional state and social productivity begin to decline; their education and training may no longer fit them for a desirable job so they may become ill and their relationship with other persons may deteriorate.

According to a survey of 500 recently retired men and women in the Boston area (National Institute of Mental Health 1976), the best adjusted retirees were involved in a major activity that they considered important, such as part-time work or participation in clubs and organizations. Most of the retired persons said they were healthy and happy. But the upper-level blue-collar workers seemed to be the best adjusted, even though they had less income than upper-level white-collar retirees. Former upper- and middle-level blue-collar workers preferred retirement, while upper- and middle-level white-collar retirees said they would rather be working. The results of this survey also indicated that preretirement counseling helps to head off adjustment difficulties and helps to identify people most likely to have problems adapting to retirement.

As a means of helping the mature adult prepare for the adjustment from work to retirement, many large businesses are providing preretirement planning and counseling programs open to employees and their spouses who are approaching the age of retirement. Most of these programs follow the American Association of Retired Persons plan and include small-group seminars, special interest groups, and private counseling for individuals with particular problems and anxieties. In addition, a rescue corps of successfully retired men and women is frequently available to help new retirees make the difficult transition from work to retirement. The small-group seminars usually consist of a short talk followed by discussion and question-answer periods. Booklets, worksheets, and bibliographies of pertinent references and local resources such as government and private agencies, clinics, doctors, and lawyers that can best assist the retiree are provided. Participants in the small-group seminars are encouraged to work together in finding additional information on matters of mutual interest. Such topics as Social Security, Medicare, Medicaid, legal affairs (including wills), family relations, housing, creative use of leisure, and income and financial planning (including potential sources of additional income) are usually included in the small-group seminars.

Intellectual Functioning

Mental aging usually occurs later in life than physical aging. This is verified, however, by cross-sectional rather than longitudinal studies. Many extraneous circumstances can influence an individual's rate of mental decline. Emotionally, the individual's attitude is an important factor, especially if the person underestimates his or her abilities and fears criticism, thus stifling motivation and increasing the feeling of uselessness. Lack of environmental stimulation, poor physical conditioning, and educational differences can be contributing factors in the stifling of motivation and can influence mental decline. Less decline in mental efficiency is usually associated with those individuals with higher intellectual abilities as compared to those with lower levels of intellectual functioning. Because tomorrow's elderly will have more education, our future concepts, especially regarding their needs and interests, may have to change. Differences can and do exist, however, between and within individuals in regard to intellectual functioning and areas of decline in the advancing years of life. Continued use of one's intellectual abilities is the key to maintaining normal brain-functioning abilities well into later life.

Memory and Learning

Memory and learning are primary functions of the central nervous system; the ability to adapt to a changing environment is significantly dependent upon one's ability to register, retain, and recall experiences.

Although memory is not significantly influenced by aging, there are some older individuals who have poor recent but good remote memories, probably because they are not as attentive in current situations or they just may be slow in quick-thinking situations. The ability to recall is usually affected more than recognition as age progresses, primarily because more cues are needed to facilitate recall.

Learning, defined as the relative permanent modification of behavior as the result of experience, is insignificantly influenced by age, even when sensory acuity begins to decline. Differences in the ability to learn in individuals over 30 can usually be attributed to problems related to input of information to the central nervous system, perception, control of attention, motivation, and general health, especially absence of diseases that might lead to impaired function of the central nervous system. Impairment in learning, therefore, should indicate some prior incapacity or debilitating change in the individual.

In learning new tasks, the older person is usually more cautious, is in need of more time to integrate responses, and is less capable of dealing with novel material that cannot readily be integrated with earlier experiences. The younger person is usually an inventive problem solver; with aging, that person acquires routines to meet the demands of life and tends to lose inventiveness. Thus, an older individual's repertory of reponses may be adequate but stale. The ability or necessary stimulation for independent and creative thinking is lacking. Because learning is slow and laborious, older people may frequently use old and tried solutions to problems. There is some evidence to indicate that the thought processes of older adults tend toward simple associations rather than analysis. The weakness in solving abstract problems seems to be related to a reduction in the ability to generate hypotheses about the nature of a problem, a lack of an orderly checking out of the facts, and a limited ability to perform at abstract levels. This ability to reason in the form of problem-solving orientation appears to decline faster than abilities of verbal meanings and numbers.

As the complexity of the task to be learned increases, older persons require more time, are less accurate, and do not always comprehend the task. They often become confused when the task is complicated, and this militates against their ability to organize their material in a logical way. More mistakes result as the complexity of the task increases. This increased caution causes a decline in both inductive and deductive reasoning.

The intensity and duration of physiological arousal during a learning task appears to be different in older individuals and influence the acquisition or extinction of responses. Therefore, arousal and other associated variables are more important influences than the intrinsic changes in the older individual's ability to learn when deficits in learning exist.

The interference effects of task reversal or habit reversal are not affected by age. However, the early phases of learning may occur more slowly in the elderly because of the intrusive effects of a mass of irrelevant or slightly interfering previous learning. For practical purposes, therefore, the older adult may need a longer early phase to overcome interference.

In verbal or abstract learning there are small, if any, differences between old and young individuals. However, perceptual-motor tasks do show interference as age progresses. It should be noted that all of what we expect to occur as people age in the form of changes in memory and learning may be inaccurate because the research surveys used to obtain data may have measured individuals with grossly different prior learning.

The attitude toward learning itself does change with age. All things being equal, older adults are less ready to learn than they used to be. They lose the desire to learn and frequently have the tendency to solve problems on the basis of what is already known rather than to experiment with new solutions. The amount of schooling appears to be more important than age as an indicator of the ability to learn during the work life. In the retirement years, differences in the ability to learn can be expected to be influenced greatly by health status and psychosocial makeup, not necessarily by factors correlated with age. It is, therefore, a myth that people over 65 are not as bright or productive as younger people. Most do have a vast fund of accumulated knowledge and keep abreast in their field of specialization.

Intellectual Abilities

The ability to adapt depends to a significant degree upon proficiency in solving problems. Successful problem solving depends upon a clear grasp of the nature of the problem facing the individual. Quite obviously, formal schooling and practical experience are important factors in determining the amount of time an individual must spend in analyzing and solving problems. Many older individuals are rigid in their solutions to problems. Changes do occur in problem-solving attitudes toward unfamiliar tasks as the interval since schooling grows. (See Memory and Learning, preceding section.)

The results of standardized intelligence tests given to adults over their life spans have implications about aging and mental performance. The patterns of these test scores definitely change with age. Between the ages of 20 and 60 general information, verbal comprehension, vocabulary, and arithmetic operations tend to show increases. However, tests involving learning and the formation of new associations such as spatial perception, arrangement of geometric forms, and decoding tasks decrease. While speed of perception and mental decoding operations decline with age and are intimately correlated to age, information items, which normally increase with age, show the greatest correlation to health status in older adults. Decline in the ability to think is clearly related to brain damage rather than aging, and test changes in information items on intelligence tests can indicate cerebrovascular brain damage, cardiovascular disease, or functional disturbances elsewhere in the body.

In recent studies of intellectual functioning conducted by Dr. Lissy F. Jarvik, professor of psychiatry at the University of California at Los Angeles, it was found that generally there is no decline either in knowledge or reasoning ability in the thirties and forties, or even in the sixties, seventies, and eighties. In one study, individuals examined after age 60, and then followed along into their seventies and eighties, showed no intellectual decline, though with advancing age it took longer to perform intellectual functions. Although older people commonly complain of poor memory, laboratory studies show that many of the old actually can learn as well as younger people and their memory is often equal. Much of what is called memory loss may really be due to inadequate learning caused by hearing difficulty, impaired vision, inattention, and similar factors. Frequently, according to Dr. Jarvik, what is misdiagnosed as mental deterioration in the elderly is really a symptom of depression. The deterioration can be overcome simply by counseling, psychotherapy, or the use of antidepressant medication (Jarvik 1975, p. 91).

Biological/physiological factors can, on occasion, cause rigid behavior in older adults. Rigidity or a "not inclined to change" approach to life's situations is said to be related to the extent of schooling and the number of years that have passed since attending school, not to aging. It is speculated that there is a correlation between intelligence and rigidity; a person of high intelligence is apt to be mentally more flexible and less rigid. Regarding mental rigidity, men tend to be more flexible than women primarily because of their former work patterns. The changing employment trend of females may alter this pattern in the future.

Many older individuals have a tendency to reminisce or think and talk about the past. This is especially true of the poorly adjusted. Individuals in their seventies or eighties can be considered childish when they frequently exhibit forgetfulness, slowness of comprehension, emotional immaturity, and animistic tendencies to live in the past. Reminiscing about the past, however, is important to many old people's happiness because these recollections fulfill deep emotional needs during the last years of life.

There is a definite positive side to growing old. The elderly may be judged superior if life experience, maturity of judgment, and accumulation of knowledge are relied upon to define achievement. The physical capacity of the elderly may be less, but their psychological and social skills may be ripe. Although some older individuals lag in psychomotor performance, many excel in information, comprehension, and verbalization. There is, therefore, evidence against the myth that impairments of memory and learning abilities are normal concomitants of aging. Aging alone has little effect on learning ability. If such impairment does exist, it is the result of prior incapacity or debilitating health change in the individual.

Personality

Although difficult to define, personality usually refers to the distinctive styles or characteristic ways in which individuals behave, react, or respond to life situations as influenced by their individual system of personal values. These patterns of response can be more or less adaptive. Reactions to developmental situations, such as retirement, and bodily changes and disease are functions of an individual's personality. The evolving personality or habit system of the individual imposes a bias or type of control over behavior. With advancing age, the adult shows a reduction in drive level that includes reduced spontaneous physical activity and reduced sexual behavior. The individual may react to these changes with increased motivation or passive retreat. After age 60 there appears to emerge a quality of effective emotional detachment from the environment. Older persons tend to have less emotion or ego involvement in their roles and activities than they had earlier in life. This may be an adaptation to the fact that the environment is moving away from the individual in the sense that peers and relatives die, jobs and careers stop, and children grow up and leave home. Such disengagement may be a reflection of reduced ego energy on the part of the drive system of the individual and a lower capacity for effective involvement with the environment.

Over a life span, changes in interests, activities, and personality traits reflect long-term developmental changes in motivations and habit systems. Although personal values and vocational interests are relatively stable over the years, attitudes toward one's self change rather markedly. In fact, these traits vary more than intellectual capacities, which are considered more important in determining adaptation abilities. In addition, various physiological changes, including those in the nervous system, may dramatically affect an individual's emotional life and response patterns, placing the person in an uneasy relationship with his or her own body and developing suspicious and anxious behavior.

Research focusing on age and rigidity tends to indicate that rigidity is more closely related to the level of intellectual functioning than to the chronological age or to a personality style of resistance to change. Other studies indicate that as individuals grow older they recognize their attitudes toward earlier life problems and develop an acceptance of themselves and their past. The preretirement period is frequently accompanied by a sense of insecurity and instability; whereas in the period after retirement, the individual is less uncertain and defensive.

There are two basic methods of adapting to uncertainties in life: (1) deny their existence, or (2) work things through as events occur. There are other methods of coping with life that, although apparently pathological in character, can lead to a degree of stability and success throughout the life span. According to one research study (HEW 1970, p. 33), there are several successfully adapting personality types that may evolve after retirement.

1. The mature type, who has a constructive approach to life. This type accepts the facts of aging, adjusts well to losses, is realistic about past and present lives, and faces death with relative equanimity.
2. The rocking-chair type, who has tendencies to lean on others. This type accepts passivity, and sits and rocks without guilt.
3. The armored type, who has well-developed defenses. This type clings to middle age behavior patterns, denies aging, keeps as busy as ever, and manages to get along very well.
4. The angry type, who often is hostile. This type characteristically blames others for his or her own limitations.
5. The self-hating type, who is a poorly adjusted individual.

Older persons as a group are willing to be more candid and intimate about such matters as successes and failures, relationships with spouses, financial achievements, and issues of religion and death. Most are not lonely, but instead are bright and alert, open-minded and adaptable. As a group these individuals are more concerned about lack of money and circumstances of living than they are about death and dying. It is, therefore, a myth that all old people are bound to go downhill as they lose job, spouses, and old friends. These happenings are not devastating if the older person has a positive, hopeful attitude toward life, is interested in people and activities, finds positive replacements for such losses, and changes personal values and goals where necessary.

Sexual Activity

There is no direct relationship between aging and decline in sexual activity. With aging, changes do occur in the human organism that can affect sexual activity. These include: (1) changes in the hormone levels in the individual, (2) changes in the thresholds of the nervous-system centers controlling the elicitation of sexual behavior, and (3) changes in the long-standing habit systems established in the central nervous system over the control of sexual behavior. Individual differences do occur in relation to all of these changes, resulting in considerable differences in the sexual behavior of older individuals. According to Masters and Johnson, aging does not affect the male's ability to have an erection until well into the eighties, although he may cease to ejaculate. The main sexual problem in the aging female is a loss of lubrication and elasticity that may cause physical discomfort. Both of these changes can be cured by hormone therapy. Actually, unless there is disease or injury, sexual satisfaction can continue until death. In fact, most marriages in late years are successful because such a union provides companionship, sex, security, and satisfaction of the desire to be needed.

Mental Health

The methods used by an individual in response to changes in environment can lead to a reduction in tensions and conflicts or increase the likelihood of lasting maladjustments and even lead to mental disorder. Mental diseases may be considered as disturbances of a long-lasting functional, anatomical, or physiological nature or as transient maladjustments. Forms of deviant behavior and mental illnesses vary in their frequency with age. Generally speaking, deviant behavior in society is typified by crimes of impulse in youth and crimes of habit in old age.

One perplexing geriatric problem is the dramatic rise in suicides among white males over the age of 75. It is more than 7 times that of young adults in their early twenties. Evidence suggests that this is because the white male frequently reacts adversely to many conditions that accompany advancing age, such as illness, physical infirmity, reduced income, movement to a new residence, and lack of contact with previous colleagues, all of which are reflected in feelings of worthlessness, or a misinterpretation or overreaction to the personal implications of health change. As women receive more equality in society, the suicide trend for older females, particularly single career women, may approach the same dramatic increase as that for men.

Suicide and depression are highly age related. As older individuals are faced with repeated episodes of physical illness, bereavement, and other psychological and social losses, depressive reactions increase.

Mental illness resulting from brain disease of late life occurs more frequently but gets less clinical attention than do characteristic mental illnesses of early life and can occur as side effects of somatic illnesses, infectious diseases, or undernutrition. These mental symptoms may not disappear until some time after the original conditions are controlled. Approximately 1 to 2 percent of the population, under current standards of hospitalization, may expect to be institutionalized for mental disease for the first time late in life. Senile dementia can be expected in about 4 percent of the population and seems to occur independently of, or in combination with, preexisting diseases such as psychoneurosis, schizophrenia, or manic-depressive reactions.

Because such a small percentage of persons in the total population is institutionalized for mental illness in late life, it can be concluded that a senile pattern of brain deterioration does not commonly accompany advancing age and when it does occur it is likely to be of pathological origin rather than a normal concomitant of growing old. Geriatric psychiatry is giving more emphasis to mixed causes of mental illness in older persons, composed of a variety of functional and organic factors in addition to the interactions of the physical illness and the social environment, rather than a single diagnosis.

Behavior and Chronic Illness

Early-life behavior patterns are related to the probability of developing cardiovascular disease. Hypertension tends to occur in persons who have a restless type of motor behavior. They tend to be bothered by the inability to be active, reflecting a feeling of the pressure and urgency of time and placing time pressure on others. Currently, sufficient information is not available regarding the causal relationship between early behavior patterns and chronic-illness outcomes. It is known, however, that stress in bereavement, especially during the first or second year after the loss of a mate, seriously taxes the individual's physiological limits, especially where there are preexisting health problems. Therefore, bereavement control measures cushioning the physiological and psychological consequences in older persons, especially in relatively isolated individuals, should be emphasized.

The Terminal Phase of Life

The terminal phase of life, accompanied by knowledge of the existence of a chronic and fatal illness, can occur in the fifties, sixties, seventies, eighties, and older or younger years of life. Individual reactions to these issues can be quite varied, ranging from complete acceptance to complete denial. The very old individual usually accepts death as inevitable; others may have difficulty adjusting to this inevitability. Regardless of the age of the individual, the strongest need at this time is to not be left alone when death does occur.

An extensive study of individuals brought back from near death indicates that "death is an indescribably wonderful sensation" that is perceived as an immediate separation of a spiritlike self-entity from the body and is accompanied by a great feeling of peace and ease.

There is a role for the health professionals in helping individuals die with dignity. The dying should not be isolated since death is a process and not an event. Instead, access to others and to the information of a normal environment should be provided.

SELECTED REFERENCES

Berkowitz, B. Changes in intellect with age: IV. Changes in achievement and survival in older people. *Journal of Genetic Psychology*, 1965, *107*, 3-14

Comfort, Alex. Sex author turns to aging. *Salt Lake Tribune*, January 27, 1975.

Hoffman, Betty H. Growing old is not the same as being old. *Woman's Day*, September 1974, 50-52, 150, 175.

Hurlock, Elizabeth B. *Developmental psychology.* 3rd ed. New York: McGraw-Hill, 1968.

Jarvik, Lissy F. Intellectual functioning. *American Family Physician*, 1975, *10*, no. 6, 91.

Kassel, Victor. Sex is for the aged also, says Salt Lake physician. *Salt Lake Tribune*, May 18, 1975.

Kinsey, A.; Pomeroy, W.; and Martin, C. *Sexual behavior in the human male.* Philadelphia: Saunders, 1948.

Kinsey, A.; Pomeroy, W.; Martin, C.; and Gebhard, P. *Sexual behavior in the human female.* Philadelphia: Saunders, 1953.

Parker, E. *The seven ages of woman.* Baltimore: Johns Hopkins, 1961.

United States Department of Health, Education and Welfare. *Working with older people: Biological, psychological, and sociological aspects of aging.* Washington, D.C.: U.S. Government Printing Office, Publication 1459, 1970.

United States Department of Health, Education and Welfare, National Institute of Mental Health. *Retirement patterns and predictions.* Washington, D.C.: U.S. Government Printing Office, Publication 1724, 1976.

4
SOCIOLOGICAL ASPECTS OF AGING

Grow old along with me!
The best is yet to be,
The last of life, for which the
first was made.
—Robert Browning

According to sociologists, a person is old when society defines him as "old". In the United States this usually means old enough to retire, or age 65. Social age includes those age-related behavior patterns expected from all members of society who are of the same chronological age. For the mature adult this also includes all of the adjustments needed to make the necessary role changes associated with retirement.

The age at which individuals are considered old, quite obviously, depends upon the roles they perform in society. Athletes may be "old" in their twenties or thirties, but a symphony conductor's prime may come in the sixties. Despite the fact that older workers as a group are highly productive and dependable, they generally have less education than younger workers and may not possess the new work skills required by changes in technology. Since we are a highly technological society with an accent on youth, supply and demand for skill can make an individual old.

Therefore, the social attitude toward the roles of the elderly in society and the opportunities provided by society for their elderly are critical factors in determining the sociological aspects of aging for any culture. Social roles are determined by customs and patterns of life built up over a period of time and are greatly influenced by current economic conditions such as the availability of food and housing.

The number of aged persons in society is also a critical factor. If the number is low, they usually hold a position of high esteem in society. If, however, the number is large, their position is usually one of low esteem. Because the number of individuals in this country over age 65 is increasing and we are currently faced with critical economic problems, their level of esteem and social role in society is changing.

Aged men, in many societies, have been looked upon as experts in solving problems of life. Today, however, it is expected that aged individuals will play a decreased role in social, community, and economic affairs.

SOCIAL PROBLEMS FOR THE AGED

The aged in our society must adjust to the marked role change that occurs when they are full-fledged members of the work force on one day and the next day they are retirees. Although many large companies do have "plans for retirement clubs," the majority of older workers currently get no real help in making this role change, in contrast to the help given the "new-on-the-job" or "new-in-school" members of our society.

There are few social roles that the elderly can perform with prestige and respect, primarily because they must compete with younger people for valued roles. At the present time society has not defined specific roles for the aged, nor developed expectations for them. In addition, many mature adults do not possess the necessary resourcefulness or experience to develop new roles for themselves; this is especially true if they have been deeply involved and dedicated to earlier life roles.

As Tuckman and Lorge (1953, p. 249) have pointed out: "Old people are living in a social climate which is not conducive to feelings of adequacy, usefulness and security, and to good adjustment in their later years."

Numerous stereotypes of the aged exist in folklore, fairy tales, mass media, and scientific studies. For example, many fairy tales depict old women as the cruel "wicked stepmother." Shakespeare has made over a hundred references to the physical and behavioral changes associated with the senescent process. In *The Seven Ages of Man* he described senility in the following words:

> *The sixth age shifts*
> *Into the lean and slipper'd pantaloon,*
> *With spectacles on nose and pouch on side,*
> *His youthful hose well sav'd a world too wide*
> *For his shrunk shank; and his big manly voice,*
> *Turning again toward childish treble, pipes*

And whistles in his sound. Last scene of all,
That ends this strange eventful history,
Is second childishness and mere oblivion,
Sans teeth, sans eyes, sans taste, sans everything.

Because most scientific studies of aging are based on institutional cases, they frequently present a negative picture of aging. A representative sample of non-institutional elderly will, in most cases, not support such negative findings.

The commonly accepted stereotypes of the aged indicate that they are (1) ineffective, (2) worn out physically and mentally, (3) crotchety, (4) hard to live with, and (5) should be pushed aside to make way for younger members of society. The aged, therefore, are treated either with tolerance and acceptance or complete rejection. Golde and Kogan (1959, p. 355) have pointed out,

> If the younger generation believes that the older generation is old-fashioned and narrow-minded and, in turn, thinks the older generation views them as wild and foolish, the inter-personal relationships that do develop will, in part, reflect these views. Furthermore, old people can hardly be expected to be totally unaware of such attitudes and beliefs.

In spite of the growing number of old people in the United States today, they occupy a minority-group status, a status which frequently excludes them from interaction with other groups in the population and which gives them little or no power. This minority-group status comes primarily from unfavorable social attitudes toward the aged that have been fostered by the unfavorable stereotypes of old age. Rosow (1962, p. 182) has pointed out,

> Their second-rate citizenship is no accident, no minor misfunctioning of our institutions and values. It is inherent in the nature of our society. Underlying the practical immediacies of health and income, the deeper human problems of old people boil down to two central issues: (1) How will we share the fruits of our abundance with them, and by what principles? (2) How can we integrate them into our society on a basis of dignity and respect? Or, simply put, how can we redeem their second-class citizenship?

The effect of second-class citizenship, as is always true for persons of minority groups, is to put the elderly on the defensive. This has a marked effect on their personal and social adjustments. It makes the latter years of life far from "golden" for most people and causes many to be victimized by the majority group. Langer (1963, p. 470) has stressed,

> If the aged are victimized in general, they are also victimized in particular. Their illness, loneliness, and terrors make the aged easy prey to a

growing army of charlatans in whom their vulnerability arouses instincts not of sympathy but of greed. An ingenious array of frauds, from quack medicines to uninhabitable homesites, and from dancing lessons to fake furnace repairs has been revealed.

The aged must adjust to decreasing strength and a gradually failing health, and they must find activities to replace customary work activities. In addition, retirement is frequently accompanied by reduced income that may necessitate a change in living arrangements. The aged frequently cannot meet social and civic obligations because of transportation, health, or financial reasons. The death of a spouse is more frequently a problem for women than for men and can further reduce income, create additional hazards from living alone, and necessitate additional changes in living arrangements.

In summary, the normal problems associated with life adjustments for the aged can frequently be complicated by additional unique problems. These problems may result from a number of factors.
1. Physical helplessness (more serious for women than men)
2. Economic insecurity which may necessitate a complete change in patterns of living
3. Feelings of rejection by society, family, or both
4. Loss of a spouse or close companion by death
5. Loss of work due to compulsory retirement

Such problems may require adjustments that evolve around changes in lifestyles and attitudes.
1. Changing living arrangements that are satisfactory despite changes in economic or physical conditions
2. Making new friends to replace lost ones
3. Developing new activities to fill increasing leisure
4. Changing attitudes toward grown children

Retirement

Retirement is the key factor around which most of the sociological aspects of aging focus. Because we live in a work-oriented society, retirement can be a socially, psychologically, and economically crippling experience for the worker. Or, if in anticipation of retirement, work roles are replaced with other roles, it can be a very positive and rewarding period. (See Psychological Aspects of Aging, chapter 3.)

Age prejudices do exist and can be the major cause of unemployment when an individual passes age 45. The Department of Employment Security today classifies anyone 45 years or more as an older worker. Age prejudices are true in all employment areas, including institutions of higher education. On April 15, 1975 at the University of Utah, during the annual meeting of the Carnegie

Foundation for the Advancement of Teaching, Alan Pifer made the following statement (Salt Lake Tribune, April 15, 1975):

> *Early retirement and other means must be found to keep the best of the younger people in academic life. Many institutions are not now in position to hire young people coming along because the spots are already filled with tenured faculty.*

One of the major problems associated with retirement is loss of income. The change from worker to retiree status cuts many incomes in half. The total pension income for persons retiring today is approximately 20 to 40 percent of the individual's former average working income. For many persons, especially widows, to be old means to be a neighbor of poverty. This is especially true today because inflation has greatly reduced the purchasing power of fixed incomes. In addition, Social Security, private pensions, and other forms of retirement income are not improving fast enough to reduce or significantly counter the present economic trends.

According to the United States Department of Health, Education and Welfare, the aggregate annual money income for the aged, including workers and retirees, is estimated to be $50 billion. But 20 percent of the older population account for 30 percent of this income. Although 1 dollar in 3 of this $50 billion comes from earnings, only a small minority of the aged are employed. In fact, 4 of 5 are not in the labor force. Of those employed, 1 in 5 is employed in part-time, low-paid employment.

AGGREGATE MONEY INCOME — AGED

32%	Earnings
30%	Social Security benefits
15%	Interest, dividends, and rents
6%	Railroad retirement and government employees retirement benefits
5%	Public assistance
5%	Miscellaneous sources
4%	Veterans' benefits
3%	Private pensions

Source: United States Department of Health, Education and Welfare, 1970.

Because retirement drastically reduces many incomes, it can also reduce participation in many activities involving membership or admission fees. Thus, expectations are reduced, activities are reduced, and, in turn, expectations drop further, especially if the personality is predisposed to it and the attitudes of others enforce it. Chronic conditions that are not necessarily limiting in a major way can become vehicles for attention, excuses for inactivity, and reasons for acting "old."

The Social Security Act of 1935 confirmed age 65 for retirement (see Federal Legislation in this chapter). This was an attempt, during the depression, to open jobs for younger workers by encouraging retirement and support of the often unemployed older worker. Since 1961 it has been possible to retire at age 62 under Social Security. This is, however, at a permanently reduced benefit rate for the worker, his spouse, and other dependents. The amount of this reduction depends on the number of months before age 65 that checks are issued to the retiree. Some private pension plans also permit retirement at age 62, and some union-management contracts (such as International Moving Lines) permit retirement at age 55.

Although some individuals retire early because of declining health and energy, or the inability to find employment, an increasing number are retiring voluntarily when their retirement income becomes available so they can enjoy their leisure. Therefore, retired individuals are getting younger, and most of them are relatively healthy members of society. In addition, because there is a trend toward early departure from the labor force, society is experiencing an increase not only in the number of old, but also in the number of *very* old citizens.

Retirement years are demanding years for the average person primarily because adjustment to retirement means adjustment to life without paid employment. In addition, it requires a change of both role and status in a youth-oriented society. Thus, the retired individual must shift from a role of independence, participation, and leadership to one of dependence, passivity, and exclusion in economic, community, and family life. This can cause the retiree to feel outdated, socially irrelevant, unwanted, and unneeded.

Retirement can mean a loss of work companionship because the individual is removed from long-time social relationships and meaningful activities. In addition, the male retiree is frequently in the way at home, which can create additional retirement problems.

At the present time Social Security, private and corporate pension plans, Medicare, Medicaid, subsidized health services, subsidized housing services, income-tax deductions, cut-rate bus fares, and other private, governmental, and voluntary efforts are society's way of supporting a growing elderly population. Social Security taxes are steadily increasing in a desperate attempt to keep pace with retirement benefits being paid out, including adjustments for the depreciated value of today's dollar. How long this tax provision for the retired will be able to keep pace with payments to retirees is one of the many concerns of the United States Senate Special Committee on Aging. Other concerns of this committee center around the following questions:

1. What is adequate retirement income?
2. What part in attaining adequate retirement income should be played by governmental programs, voluntary group action, individual effort?
3. Is the economic problem of aging a temporary problem that requires a different solution today than it will in the future?
4. Who shall support the elderly?
5. How shall they be supported?
6. Is their welfare a public-assistance problem or a social right?

Housing

Housing is an important aspect of life for the mature adult primarily because, with advancing age, an increasing amount of time is spent in the home. Many mature adults want to live alone for the needed feeling of self-reliance, dignity, and self-sufficiency provided by such living arrangements. In addition, the light housekeeping and gardening associated with living alone contribute to the exercise needs and occupy potentially lonely hours.

More than 66.6 percent of America's elderly remain in the communities where they have lived most of their lives and in the same homes. Seventy percent own their own homes and prefer to live there for economic and emotional reasons and because they prefer the security provided by the familiar surroundings. Because utilities, taxes, and home-repair costs are sharply rising, financial burdens are increasing for the elderly living in their own homes. These increased costs are necessitating moves for many elderly into public low-rent housing especially designed for the aged, furnished rooms, or old downtown hotels and boarding houses that have been converted into residential facilities catering exclusively to the aged. Many of these boarding houses and residential facilities for the aged include meals and visiting housekeepers as part of the rent. Many locals communities provide Meals on Wheels and visiting nursing services to the aged living alone. Some elderly do move in with their children when they can no longer support themselves. But this is infrequent because the modern family, in its present form, is not equipped to care for old persons or does not have adequate living space. When all alternatives to housing have been exhausted and, in most cases, as a last resort, the elderly individual either enters a nursing home voluntarily or is sent there by the family.

This wide variation in living arrangements can present a real challenge to the community recreation specialist, especially when other factors, such as transportation and money, influence mobility. See Community Recreation Programs (chapter 9) for additional information.

For the estimated 500,000 elderly with adequate incomes there is a current trend toward movement into retirement communities which have mushroomed primarily in Florida and the Southwest. In 1975 such property could be leased or bought for approximately $27,000 to $28,000. These living units contain standardized accommodations designed for the older person, such as bathrooms with grab bars, floor plans without steps or protruding obstacles, and entrances that permit the free movement of wheelchairs. In addition, most retirement communities offer their residents recreation and social activities. Many retirement communities exclude younger people (no one under 50 can buy or lease property), ban dogs, put a time limit on visits by children, exclude child residents, have their own security police, and have prepaid health insurance included in the monthly rental or mortgage payments. Frequently, retirees move into retirement communities to escape problems such as robbery, mugging, and strain of noise associated with living in big cities. As one 84-year-old resident living in a retirement community said (*Time*, June 2, 1975, p. 45),

> *We were robbed three times in a period of four years, and my wife was mugged by two youths in front of our front door. Children bounced a basketball against the walls of the house until it drove us crazy. I didn't realize the strain until we moved here; now I can take a walk at midnight in safety. Here we can not only enjoy a whole range of activities with other elderly people, I can also find the peace and quiet so necessary for my work, which is etching.*

Nursing Homes

Approximately 5 percent or 1.5 million older Americans are in nursing homes (long-term care facilities). According to the law, persons admitted to nursing homes must be referred by a physician who has diagnosed the medical problem and outlined the care needed by the patient. In addition, a medical follow-up by a physician is required. According to the United States Senate Special Committee on Aging, these are the major factors concerning the nursing-home population:

1. Most residents are very old, with an average age of 82. Although 95 percent are over age 65, 70 percent are over age 70.
2. Women outnumber men three to one, and 63 percent of these women are widowed.
3. The residents are alone. Almost 50 percent have no viable relationship with a close relative, and 30 percent have only collateral relatives near their own age. Therefore, most patients do not have visitors. In addition, there is little evidence to support the theory that families "dump" their aged into nursing homes.

4. More than 55 percent come from their own or relatives' homes, 32 percent come from hospitals (22 percent from general and 10 percent from state mental hospitals), and 13 percent come from other nursing homes, homes for the aged, boarding homes, or other housing.

5. The length of stay in a nursing home is two or more years. Conservative figures indicate that 50 percent of nursing-home patients die in nursing homes, 21 percent are returned to hospitals, 19 percent are sent home or to their relatives' homes, and 10 percent are placed in other accommodations.

6. Chronic or crippling disabilities are common in nursing-home patients. Sixty-five percent suffer from cardiovascular disease, 20 percent suffer from what is loosely termed senility. Fractures rank third most prevalent at 11 percent, followed by arthritis at 10 percent. Large quantities of drugs are taken for these conditions.

7. Fifty-five percent are mentally impaired (see no. 4).

8. Less than 50 percent are ambulatory, 55 percent require assistance in bathing, 47 percent need help in dressing, 11 percent in eating, and 33 percent are incontinent.

9. Most nursing-home patients are placed in facilities less than 25 miles from their community home.

10. Many older Americans regard nursing homes with fear and hostility, and there are sharp increases in death rate associated with transfer to nursing homes. This phenomenon is termed "transplantation shock" and is associated with the fact that there is a negative relationship between survival and institutionalization, as many old people believe entry into a home is a prelude to death.

Although there are many excellent nursing homes across the nation, the nursing-home scandals of the 1960s and 1970s publically exposed widespread evidence of overdrugging of patients, inadequate diets, poor rehabilitation programs, and violations of federal and state regulations in many nursing homes (HEW, cited in *Time*, June 2, 1975). As a result, improvements are being made in federal and state inspection and law-enforcement procedures for these long-term care facilities. Particular attention is being given to those laws designed to eliminate abuse in nursing homes. In addition, many nursing homes have lost their licenses to operate; others have made vast improvements in their operating procedures.

The following guidelines may be useful in the selection of a long-term care facility for an aged person:

1. Become fully acquainted with the various classifications of homes that are available, and the types of services they provide.

   a. Skilled nursing home or comprehensive home. This facility is staffed and equipped to provide skilled nursing care under the direction of a physician or registered nurse, who is prepared to exercise professional nursing judgment in evaluating the patient's condition and in providing appropriate care. Some of the tasks performed in this home include administration of tube feedings and other special procedures ordered by the attending physician.

   b. Intermediate nursing home. This convalescent center is staffed and equipped to provide technical nursing, by or under the supervision of a licensed practical nurse. There is a doctor on call for consultation. The licensed practical nurse is able to care for patients whose conditions are relatively stable, and for whom planned patterns of nursing care have been developed. This can include injections, sterile dressing changes, and administration of medications.

   c. Personal care home. This facility is staffed and equipped to provide personal care by or under the direct supervision of a nursing assistant. Services include help with walking, dressing, eating, getting in and out of bed, and bathing.

2. Consult with the patient's physician to determine the type of facility needed.

3. Visit a select group of nursing homes for a close, analytical look at the way nurses and aides treat the elderly patients and the other types of services provided.

Federal rules and regulations for operators of nursing homes require nursing homes to employ a full-time activity director for the leisure hours of residents. Thus, a new challenge has been created for the recreation specialist. (See Programming for Extended-Care Facilities, chapter 10, for additional information.)

FEDERAL LEGISLATION

Since the Social Security Act of 1935, an increasing amount of legislation has been enacted for the benefit of the retired and elderly.

Social Security

The Social Security Act of 1935 has been amended over the years in an attempt to keep pace with changing economic trends and to improve protection for workers and their families. In 1935 this act covered only the worker upon retirement and extended to only industrial and commercial employees. The 1939 amendments extended payments to the survivors upon a worker's death and to certain dependents upon retirement. Then, in 1950, coverage was extended to include most self-employed persons, most state and local employees, household and farm employees, members of the Armed Forces, and clergymen. Today almost all jobs in the United States are covered by Social Security.

In 1954 disability insurance was added to Social Security to give workers protection against loss of earnings due to total disability. Then, in 1965, Medicare was enacted under the Social Security Act to assure hospital and medical-insurance protection to people 65 and over. As a result of legislation enacted in 1972, Social Security benefits will increase automatically as the consumer price index increases. Regardless of age at retirement, and up to the age of 72, persons on Social Security must report income, other than Social Security benefits, of $2,760 and higher annually.

MONTHLY SOCIAL SECURITY BENEFITS FOR 1975

	Average	Minimum	Maximum
Retired worker	$181	$ 93.80	$304.10
Retired couple	$310	$140.70	$457.40

To help cover the increasing Social Security benefits to retirees, deductions paid by the wage earner have increased over the years to a maximum of $895.05 in 1976. A continuously updated manual, *Your Social Security,* is available free at any Social Security office and is automatically mailed to retiring individuals. This manual contains detailed information on all aspects of Social Security rights, responsibilities, and benefits.

Supplemental Security Income

The Supplemental Security Income Program for the aged, blind, and disabled (SSI) became effective under the Social Security Act, January 1, 1974. This program replaces the state-administered assistance payments to the needy aged, blind, and disabled and guarantees them a total 1976 income of at least $150 per month for individuals and $230 per month for couples. As with other federal legislation, this law has been improved since its passage to assure that the income of the needy aged, blind, and disabled keeps pace with cost-of-living increases.

Effective October 1974, this law also exempts from consideration as unearned income for SSI purposes, support and maintenance payments made by a nonprofit organization on behalf of an SSI beneficiary residing in a nonprofit retirement home or similar residential institution, or furnished directly by the institution "unless such institution has expressly undertaken an obligation to furnish full support and maintenance to such individual or spouse without any current or future payment therefor" (Public Law 93-484). Thus, subject to the above exception, the subsidized portion of an SSI beneficiary's maintenance in a nonprofit home for the aged or similar facility is not considered as unearned income and does not reduce or eliminate that individual's SSI payments.

Recipients of Supplemental Security Income are eligible to receive food stamps except in five states where the recipients receive the cash value of those stamps. Other SSI benefits to the elderly include the following:

1. Exclusion of the value of a home from consideration as a resource. Current regulations exclude the value of a home up to $25,000 in the Continental United States and up to $35,000 in Alaska and Hawaii.
2. Authorization of full SSI benefits during the first four months of a recipient's institutionalization.
3. Authorization of a subsidy by private, nonprofit organizations of a recipient's support outside of a home for the aged or similar residential facility.
4. Exclusion of rent supplements from consideration as income or resources under the Housing and Community Development Act of 1974.
5. Provision of a cash housing allowance, in the amount by which rent exceeds 33.3 percent of a recipient's total monthly income, up to $50 a month. Items that would be counted as expenses are rent or mortgage payments, real estate taxes, expenses for gas and electric utilities, and home and water heating. The rate of benefit would be the lesser of two levels: $600 per year, or the amount by which an individual's housing expenses exceed 33.3 percent of his annual income.
6. Reduction by 20 percent in the amount of monthly benefits of a recipient living in the household of another.

Recipients of Supplemental Security Income are also eligible for social services. Under the Social Security Act (October 1, 1975), the goals of social services to the aged include: self-support, self-sufficiency, protective services to preserve or reunite families, prevention or reduction of inappropriate institutional care by providing community-based and home-based care, and referral or admission to institutional care where appropriate. Examples of social services to the aged would be: services relating to the management and maintenance of the home; day-care services; transportation services; training and related services; information, referral, and counseling services; preparation and delivery of meals; health support services; and appropriate combinations of services designed to meet the specific needs of the aged.

Medicare

Persons 65 and older are eligible for Medicare hospital and medical-insurance protection. The hospital insurance part of Medicare helps pay the cost of inpatient hospital care and certain kinds of follow-up care. There is no fee to Social Security recipients for this hospital insurance unless they have not worked long enough to be eligible. In this case a monthly premium of $40 is required. Medicare hospital-insurance recipients are responsible for the first $104 of their hospital bill during the first 60 days of hospital care in each benefit period.

Medicare pays the rest of the costs of covered services for the first 60 days and for an additional 30 days subject to a daily coinsurance payment. The law requires an annual review of hospital costs under Medicare and an adjustment of the portion of the bill for which a Medicare beneficiary is responsible if these costs have risen substantially.

The medical-insurance part of Medicare helps pay the costs of physician's services, outpatient hospital services, and certain other medical items and services not covered by hospital insurance. Recipients pay a basic annual premium of $93.60 for this coverage ($7.80 per month). Increases in these premiums are limited to the percentage by which Social Security cash benefits increase. A leaflet, *A Brief Explanation of Medicare,* is available at all Social Security offices and contains detailed information on Medicare coverage.

Medicaid

Medicaid pays all medical expenses not covered by Medicare, including drugs, to the elderly who do not have sufficient assets or income to support themselves. Under the Medicaid regulations, all support voluntarily given the aged is counted the same way as if it were income for that person. An individual must be considered at or near the poverty level to be eligible for Medicaid and other forms of public aid.

Veterans' Benefits

By law, veterans receive financial support and medical care from the federal government. Veterans' Administration facilities throughout the country include medical and psychiatric hospitals, domiciliary care facilities, nursing homes, and outpatient clinics. The Veterans' Administration states that it has the most comprehensive program for continued treatment and follow-up of the aging patient to be found anywhere in the free world.

Older Americans Act

The Older Americans Act of 1965, an outgrowth of the 1961 White House Conference on Aging, was created to engage older people in community-action projects and voluntary services. This has been accomplished through the following National Older American Service Programs:
1. Foster Grandparents Program which pays oldsters for supervising dependent and neglected youngsters
2. Retired Senior Volunteer Program (RSVP) which pays out-of-pocket expenses to aged involved in community activities such as entertaining the handicapped and visiting homebound patients
3. Senior Corps of Retired Executives (SCORE) which reimburses retired executives for expenses incurred while counseling small businesses and community organizations

4. Senior Companions Program which reimburses retirees for out-of-pocket expenses incurred while visiting homebound, nursing-home, hospital, and institutionalized aged

The Older Americans Act established the Administration on Aging and stimulated the 1971 White House Conference on Aging. In addition, it established the Older Americans Community Service Employment Act for the purpose of providing part-time community service employment to low-income individuals aged 55 or older in public-service projects or projects other than construction operated by tax-exempt organizations on a nonsectarian basis. Community-service employment is defined as social, health, welfare, education, library, recreation, and other similar services; conservation, maintenance, or restoration of natural resources; community betterment or beautification; and antipollution and environmental quality efforts. This act also prohibits discrimination against individuals on account of age in any program or activity receiving federal financial assistance, except in programs specifically designed for individuals in certain age groups.

Additional services to the aged under the Older Americans Act include the following services:

1. Nutrition Services. This section establishes local nutrition centers which provide low-cost hot meals and companionship to the aged and Meals-on-Wheels vans that deliver hot food directly to the doors of the homebound aged. The Secretary of Agriculture has the authority to purchase meat, poultry, and dairy products for use in these nutrition centers. In addition, supportive transportation is provided in connection with nutrition projects.

2. Transportation Services. This section authorizes the various states to meet the transportation needs of older Americans through the development of low-cost, individualized, flexible transportation projects which will provide increased access to nutrition projects, health and medical-care facilities, and social, recreational, and cultural activities. Authorization is provided for the pooling of the various state-agencies financial resources to cover the costs of transportation services to meet the common needs of individuals served under these programs. Priority is to be given to assuring transportation services in areas where public transportation is inadequate.

3. Special Service Programs for the Elderly. These special services include homemaker and other home services, legal and other counseling assistance, residential repair and renovation, transportation, and home-mortgage interest reduction and insurance payments for low-income individuals 60 years of age and older. State agencies on aging are authorized: (*a*) to disburse funds to any public or private nonprofit agency that will provide older persons with homemaker services, home health services, shopping services, escort services, reader services, letter-writing services, or other

services designed to assist such persons in leading a more independent life and to enable such persons to continue living independently in a home environment without the need for institutionalization; (b) to disburse funds to public and private nonprofit organizations for legal and other counseling services and assistance, including tax counseling and assistance, and financial counseling to assist elderly persons living in nursing homes to meet problems and needs arising out of the manner in which such homes are administered, to train lawyers, lay advocates, and paraprofessional persons, to develop law-school curricula and clinical-education programs which address the problems and needs of elderly persons, and to provide such other information, training, or assistance as may be necessary to meet such problems and needs; (c) to disburse funds to any public or private nonprofit organization or institution for residential repairs and renovations, to enable elderly persons, through financial assistance or otherwise, to make such repairs and renovations with respect to their homes as may be necessary for such homes to meet minimum housing standards; or to adapt existing housing, or construction of new housing, to meet the needs of elderly persons suffering from physical disabilities; and (d) to provide services to improve the physical and mental health of the elderly through programs of regular physical activity and exercise.

4. Model Projects. This section provides for ombudsman activities for nursing-home residents, improvement of services to low-income and minority groups, and the establishment and operation of day-care centers for the ambulatory elderly.

National Institute on Aging

In June of 1974 the Department of Health, Education and Welfare created a National Institute on Aging and appointed a National Advisory Council on Aging to set the policies and state the missions and interests of this institute. One of the primary functions of the National Institute on Aging is the promotion of research related to the psychological, sociological, biological, and physiological aspects of aging.

Health Legislation

Under the Health Services and Nurse Training Amendments of 1975, authorization has been given for the establishment of a Committee on Mental Health and Illness of the Elderly. The function of this committee is to advise the legislators regarding: (1) the future needs for mental-health facilities, personnel, research, and training to meet the mental-health needs of the elderly; and (2) the appropriate care of elderly persons who have been institutionalized.

SOCIOLOGICAL FACTORS AND LEISURE

For the mature adult, social adjustments, changes in interests, and use of leisure time are all interrelated. Although it is assumed that older individuals usually do not develop new interests, but instead concentrate on those acquired when they were younger, especially those in which they have maintained continued involvement and which provide the greatest satisfaction, numerous sociological factors can influence choice of activity. Although the majority of mature adults will have few social-adjustment problems, others will be confronted with many.

Early retirement and increased longevity can remove many of the demands from an individual's life. When this is combined with the loss of a spouse or other close "activity" companion, the individual's day may frequently become a series of long and lonely hours that may be difficult to fill with satisfying experiences. It is important that substitute companions and activities be found to fill the days so that the individual can maintain a healthy mental outlook and not use daydreaming and reminiscing as a means of escape. This provides a yet unmet challenge to community recreation agencies: how to attract these individuals into programs? And how to provide them with satisfying, rewarding experiences so they will want to return?

Although lack of money may not cause as serious an adjustment as loss of companionship, it can prevent an individual from participating in many favorite activities because of inability to pay the admission fees; to purchase tickets, equipment, or supplies; or to pay bus fares. Some community-recreation agencies are helping resolve this problem by providing reduced green fees on golf courses, free life passes to long-time participants, craft supplies at nominal fees, and reduced bus fares. If and when such fee reductions are available, they should be publicized so that all interested senior citizens can benefit from such services. If such reductions are not available, community-recreation agencies must provide substitute activities that will satisfy the leisure-time needs of this group.

Failing health, lack of energy, limited mobility, and a decrease in sensory acuity can frequently necessitate a change in choice of activity, creating an increase in sedentary pursuits and a decrease in strength and energy-type activities. This does not mean that the recreation specialist should return the aged adult to childlike activities, but it does necessitate the adaptation of satisfying activities to the new limitations of the individual.

Sociologists will agree that social class and cultural backgrounds influence the variety of activities and amount of time spent on them by the various segments of our population. As a group, individuals in higher social levels belong to more clubs and other community and religious organizations, travel more, have a greater variety of interests, and spend more time and money on recreation than people in lower social levels. In addition, women, especially those in the higher socioeconomic levels, have a wider range of recreational interests than men or other working women. A problem, however, frequently occurs when retirement income drastically reduces the purchasing power for club memberships, and "not being able to keep up with the Joneses" in the area of club membership and dress creates a serious adjustment problem in role and status.

For many segments of our population, cultural backgrounds and close family relationships have developed and fostered leisure participation patterns that center around the home and immediate neighborhood. This may explain why many senior citizens do not participate in community-center recreational activities, preferring to remain in the immediate neighborhood during their leisure hours.

Because the retired members of society represent a very diverse group, appropriate recreational services must include a wide variety of activities.

1. Activities which afford status, recognition, and achievement.
2. Activities which provide a social group as a replacement for former co-workers and companions.
3. Activities which include a variety of interests directly related to adjustments.
4. Activities which develop positive attitudes toward leisure pursuits.
5. Activities which provide meaningful expression to self and others or are creative in terms of traditional and contemporary social values.
6. Activities which contain aspects of work. This is especially important for the individual whose life previously focused on work-related activities. This would include hobbies which are useful or can be sold. According to one senior citizen: "Hobbies are eccentric when you never make anything (useful) out of them or get anything (monetary) out of them."
7. Activities which are recurrent, organized, visible to a social audience, permit a range of participation, and foster the formation of new roles.

The most common recreational interests of the aged include visiting friends, reading newspapers and magazines, watching television, gardening, sewing, and participating in civic, church, adult education, Golden Age Clubs, and other senior-citizen organizations. Although relatively few participate actively, this trend is changing as the number of early retirees increases, especially for members of retirement communities where a variety of sports and other amusements are readily available to residents.

The remainder of this text contains detailed information on planning, organizing, and conducting appropriate recreational activities for this diverse segment of our population—the mature adults.

SELECTED REFERENCES

Golde, P., and Kogan, N. A sentence completion procedure for assessing attitudes toward old people. *Journal of Gerontology,* 1959, *14,* 355-363.

Hurlock, Elizabeth B. *Developmental psychology.* 3rd ed. New York: McGraw-Hill, 1968.

Langer, E. Growing old in America: Frauds, quackery swindle the aged and compound their troubles. *Science,* 1963, *140,* 470-472.

Pifer, Alan. Meeting of the Carnegie Foundation for the Advancement of Teaching. *Salt Lake Tribune,* April 15, 1975.

Rosow, I. Old age: One moral dilemma of an affluent society. *Gerontologist,* 1962, *2,* 182-191.

Schloss, Irvin P., ed. *Washington Report.* New York: American Foundation for the Blind, December 1975.

Schloss, Irvin P., ed. *Washington Report.* New York: American Foundation for the Blind, February 1976.

Shaughnessy, Mary E. The role of the medical director in the nursing home. *Journal of the American Geriatrics Society,* 1973, *21,* 569-571.

Time Magazine. New outlook for the aged. June 2, 1975, 44-49.

Tuckman, J., and Lorge, I. Attitudes toward old people. *Journal of Social Psychology,* 1953, *37,* 249-260.

United States Department of Health, Education and Welfare. *Working with older people: Biological, psychological, and sociological aspects of aging.* Washington, D.C.: U.S. Government Printing Office, Publication 1459, 1970.

United States Senate Special Committee on Aging. *Long term care facility improvement study.* Washington, D.C.: U.S. Government Printing Office, 1975.

United States Senate Special Committee on Aging. *Nursing home care in the United States: Failure in public policy.* Washington, D.C.: U.S. Government Printing Office, 1974.

5
THERAPEUTIC INTERVENTION

Health must be one of the joys of life as no other joy is possible without it.
—Thomas More

During the past two decades, the field of geriatrics has been dominated by two theories that attempt to explain the process whereby the mature adult either adjusts or fails to adjust adequately to the reality of aging: the Role-Flexibility Theory and the Disengagement Theory.

In 1954 Robert J. Havinghurst developed his Role-Flexibility Theory based on the idea that active involvement is the key to successful adjustment and the chosen mode for the aging and that disengagement is not a self-selected way of life. His research indicated that individuals who were highly active in a given social role were more likely to be happy and to make a good social adjustment to old age than those who were less active. With advanced age an individual's activities may be intensified, assumed, reduced, or discontinued for the first time. The ability to change activity roles and select new activities that provide status, achievement, and recognition is important if the aging individual is to maintain a high level of life satisfaction. For most mature adults the set of habits that constitutes a role is changed only with difficulty. To change roles easily and increase or reduce activity in a given role requires a personal quality which Havinghurst calls role flexibility. To acquire this quality, one must cultivate a successful variety of role experiences. This must be done throughout life by developing various interests and goals that are strong but not rigid. With developed activities that have a continuing value over a lifetime, the mature adult will slide easily into the retirement stage of life without major difficulties.

Elaine Cumming's and W. E. Henry's Disengagement Theory was formulated in 1961 when their work began to indicate that many of the older individuals in their program seemed to be less involved with other people and accepted or even welcomed comparative isolation. As a result, they theorized that aging individuals naturally and voluntarily withdraw from too great an involvement with others, cut down on their overall social and emotional investments, tend to surrender many of their social roles, and seem to become satisfied with only casual, superficial social contacts. They concluded that disengagement was an inevitable process resulting from the acceptance of such probabilities as death, declining health, and low socioeconomic status. Their contention was that disengagement was a purposeful withdrawal from active roles; the individual was motivated by the beginning of preparation for these potential realities. Time and rate of disengagement vary among individuals, but the theorists state that the process becomes self-perpetuating once it has begun. Disengagement occurs only when individuals sense a lack of social measuring devices in their lives, such as societal pressures to retire, and can be warded off if the ability to maintain such devices is retained. If and when mature adults sense that these qualities are slipping from them, the decision between retirement or functioning in a different sphere becomes imminent. Once mature adults begin to perceive themselves as old, because their knowledge and skills are declining, they may begin the disengagement process on their own volition.

The Disengagement Theory states that the process of withdrawal may be initiated by the individual, society, or both. If the two factors exert simultaneous pressure, a successful disengagement will follow. If, however, the societal pressure appears before the individual is ready to withdraw, the person is likely to experience a significant decline in morale. This latter possibility can produce a traumatic effect if the aging individual's self-concept and success evolve around the roles from which there is involuntary disengagement. However, there still can be a successful adjustment to the disengaged state if suitable new roles are substituted for those that have been lost. Cumming and Henry suggest that people who disengage on their own initiative tend to have higher morale than those who do not. They also discovered that the least disengaged were of quite high morale. The problems tend to come in the intermediate process of disengagement and cause many cases of poor or disjunctive adjustment.

According to Kraus (1973), the Disengagement Theory discourages attempts by society to keep older persons alert and active through recreational, social, and service activities. As stated by sociologist Chad Gordon (1970, p. 23),

> *Disengagement theory is a rationalization for the fact that old people haven't a damn thing to do, and nothing to do it with.*

Regardless of how we define adjustment to the processes of aging, those individuals who do not adequately adjust or develop related maladjustment problems may be in need of special rehabilitation services. It is estimated that only 2 percent of the aging population are in need of extensive psychological rehabilitation.

Currently, a variety of rehabilitation approaches are being used, singly or in various combinations, with the hospitalized or institutionalized geriatric patient. Because the entire staff must cooperate in the total rehabilitation process, the recreator working in geriatrics should be familiar with the various rehabilitation approaches included in this chapter.

REALITY THERAPY

Reality Therapy, as an approach to psychiatry, was developed during the early 60s by G. L. Harrington, M.D. and William Glasser, M.D. Reality Therapy stresses reality, responsibility, and right and wrong behavior. It is based on the supposition that, from birth to death, all human beings have two basic needs:

1. The need to love and be loved. This need for love ranges from friendship, through mother love, family love, and conjugal love.
2. The need to feel that we are worthwhile to ourselves and to others. This need usually accompanies the need to love and be loved. All human beings must maintain a satisfactory standard of behavior and must evaluate and improve their own conduct regarding morals, standards, values, and right and wrong behavior.

According to Glasser (1975, p. viii),

> *To be worthwhile we must maintain a satisfactory standard of behavior. To do so we must learn to correct ourselves when we do wrong and to credit ourselves when we do right. If we do not evaluate our own behavior or, having evaluated it, if we do not act to improve our conduct where it is below our standards, we will not fulfill our needs to be worthwhile and will suffer as acutely as when we fail to love or be loved. Morals, standards, values, or right and wrong behavior are all intimately related to the fulfillment of our needs for self-worth and are . . . a necessary part of Reality Therapy.*

Although the ability to fulfill these two basic needs may vary from individual to individual, they are the same for everyone. To fulfill these needs, we must be involved with people; at all times in our lives, we must have at least *one* person who cares about us and for whom we care. This one person also must be in touch with reality and be able to fulfill his or her own needs within the world.

Thus, essential to fulfillment of our needs is a person, preferably a group of people, with whom we are emotionally involved from the time we are born to the time we die. According to Glasser (1975, p. 8) "Much of what we call senility or senile psychosis is nothing more than the reaction of aged people to isolation." They may be physically near but no longer involved with people. Everyone must be sufficiently involved with people to fulfill their needs. The bedridden, senile aged can become vigorous, self-sufficient and active again through the use of Reality Therapy.

Responsibility, a concept basic to Reality Therapy, is defined as the ability to fulfill one's needs, and to do so in a way that does not deprive others of the ability to fulfill their needs. A responsible person's activities give that individual a feeling of self-worth and a feeling of being worthwhile to others. The person is motivated to strive, and perhaps endure privation, to attain self-worth. Irresponsible people may or may not do what they say, depending upon how they feel, the effort they have to make, and what is in it for them. They gain neither our respect nor their own, and, in time, they will suffer or cause others to suffer as a result of their irresponsible behavior.

Responsibility and the ability to fulfill one's needs are not inherent; they must be learned or developed continuously from the beginning to the end of life through involvement with responsible fellow human beings.

According to the philosophy of Reality Therapy, the cause of most psychiatric problems, if not organic in nature, is the inability of the individual to satisfy basic human needs for relatedness and respect. In their unsuccessful effort to fulfill their needs, no matter what behavior they choose, all patients have a common characteristic: they all deny the reality of the world around them. This denial or distorting of some or all of reality, common to all patients, can be a partial denial or the total blotting out of all reality. In addition, the patient acts irresponsibly—he or she has not been and is not now living responsibly. The patient can be cured by strengthening that individual's ability to cope now with the stresses of the world by becoming responsible, by ceasing to deny the world, and by recognizing that reality exists and that personal needs must be fulfilled within its framework.

In Reality Therapy the therapist is a teacher of responsibility. *The Miracle Worker* is an example of this struggle between responsibility (Anne Sullivan, teacher) and irresponsibility (Helen Keller, pupil). The therapist or teacher of responsibility must become involved with and be very real to the patient, answering questions, suggesting ways to solve problems, and leading the patient toward reality, toward grappling successfully with the tangible and intangible aspects of the real world. The therapist must be a very responsible person—strong, interested, human, sensitive, understanding, knowledgeable, and willing to become sufficiently involved to be helpful to the patient.

A proper therapeutic involvement is essential if Reality Therapy is to be successful. This consists of a completely honest human relationship in which the patients, for perhaps the first time in their lives, realize that someone cares enough about them to accept them as they are and to help them fulfill their needs in the real world. Emphasis on patient behavior is a continuing part of this involvement. Praise should be given freely when the patient acts responsibly and disapproval should be given when he acts irresponsibly. Therapy should be in the direction of helping the patient to improve the capacity and desire to live more responsibly, prudently, and wisely and to gain greater maturity and conscientiousness. Thus, the concept of responsibility does not imply or stress the evil in people; instead, it sees and builds upon their potentialities for good. It is decidedly optimistic and hopeful rather than cynical or pessimistic.

All patients are treated almost exactly the same, individually or as a group. Group sessions are extremely effective when several patients have similar problems. All that needs to be diagnosed, regardless of the behavior expressed by the patient, is whether that person is suffering from irresponsibility or from an organic illness. The precepts and principles of Reality Therapy are the foundation of successful, satisfying social life everywhere.

The therapist must have the skill to put the responsibility for behavior change on the patients and, after involvement has been established, to ask why they remain in therapy if they are not dissatisfied with their behavior. The patients must learn to understand that they can find happiness only within themselves.

Reality Therapy is not concerned with the past; instead the therapist must become interested in and discuss all aspects of the patient's present life. These discussions should relate to the patient's behavior whenever possible, including the patient's interests, hopes, fears, opinions, and values. Through these conversations the therapist should expand the patient's range of interests and make that person aware of life beyond his or her difficulties. Discussions can be about anything—books, politics, sports, hobbies, sex, or religion. Through these discussions the patient must accomplish two objectives:

1. The patient must test the opinions of the therapist on many subjects to discover if the therapist is responsible.

2. The patient must develop an increased sense of self-worth in the process of parrying his or her convictions and values with a trusted, respected person (the therapist) who should relate discussions to what the patient is doing *now*, the reality of what the patient does to what he or she says. Discussions should relate to the patient's growing awareness that he or she is a part of the world and is perhaps able to cope with it. Any and all discussion is relevant to therapy when values, standards, and responsibilities are in the background.

The therapist must skillfully and directly stress discussion of subject matter in areas where the patient acts responsibly, showing the patient how these areas can be expanded in his everyday life. The therapist should not sympathize or excuse the patient, and excuses for behavior are not accepted. Because the past cannot be changed, all discussion should focus on the present, especially the reality of the present, stressing that the patient must become responsible *now*. The therapist should never divorce emotions and happiness from behavior and should stress what the patient is doing, not why he or she is doing it. The therapist's job is to point out the reality of what the patient is doing *now* and to search for the *why* that he or she will always grasp in an effort not to change.

Relearning is the last phase of therapy and begins when the patient admits irresponsible behavior. Following an admission of irresponsibility, better patterns of behavior can be learned. Primary importance must be given to the whole Reality Therapy process during which the patient gradually changes from irresponsible to responsible behavior.

In summary, the basic job of the Reality Therapist is to become involved with the patients and then to get them to face reality. When patients are confronted with reality by the therapist with whom they are involved, they are forced again and again to decide whether or not they wish to take responsible paths. Reality may be painful, it may be harsh, it may be dangerous, but it changes slowly. All any person can do is to struggle with it in a responsible way by doing right, enjoying the pleasure or suffering the pain that may result.

In 1962 Dr. G. L. Harrington converted the rehabilitation program of a ward for long-term hospitalized patients at the Veterans Administration Neuropsychiatric Hospital in West Los Angeles, California, into a Total Reality Program. The patients in the ward were classified as the most chronic, stable psychotic patients in the hospital, who had been unsuccessfully treated by other methods and whose current occupancy rate in the hospital remained at the maximum allowable level. The average discharge record for these patients was 2 per year, and the length of stay in the hospital for most was indefinite, averaging 15 to 24 years.

In 1962, after 1 year of a Total Reality Program, 25 patients were released; 75 patients were released in 1963. Of these 100 patients, only 3 returned to the hospital for additional treatment. In 1965, after 3 years of operation in this Total Reality Program, Dr. Harrington estimated a complete turn-over annually in the ward.

The program in this Veterans Hospital included individual and group therapy and stressed carefully graded increments of responsibility for each and every patient, permitting the patients to slowly work their way back to reality. Each patient was considered as an individual whose behavior had reflected the best that that person had been able to do up to that point. The staff did not respond to abnormal behavior and thinking but instead treated the patients as if they were capable of acting normally or more responsibly.

A continual therapeutic effort was used to involve the patient first with the staff and then with the closed-ward program. The staff used patience, humor, and persistence to force themselves into the patient's life. The staff discovered that, when little attention was paid to an increase in symptoms or withdrawal, the patients changed their behavior. The entire ward was involved in the program and mental illness was not accepted. Patients were slowly given increased responsibility. At the same time, they were shown how to improve self-help skills such as bathing, shaving, and brushing teeth. As the patients began gaining self-respect and self-worth, more emphasis was placed on constructive, realistic work activity.

Timing and judgment regarding the increase of patient responsibility were considered critical aspects of the program. In most cases, the patient knew when he or she was ready to accept more responsibility and would test the staff's judgment by asking for more responsibility than he or she was ready to handle. The final phase of this program included mainstreaming the patient into the community, whereby the person lived in society and worked in the hospital for several months before being released.

According to Dr. Harrington, there are three advantages of a Total Reality Therapy Program over conventional therapeutic methods: (1) it is less expensive; (2) it takes less time; and (3) it is 90 percent successful. The Institute for Reality Therapy, 11633 San Vicente Boulevard, Los Angeles, California 90049, offers a training program in this rehabilitation technique.

REALITY ORIENTATION AND REMOTIVATION

Although Reality Therapy and Reality Orientation both imply reality, they are quite different therapeutic approaches to rehabilitation. Reality Therapy stresses a development of responsibility within the patient in relation to the reality of what is acceptable as right or wrong behavior. Reality Orientation and Remotivation consist of a series of continuous processes designed to help confused or disoriented patients relearn basic current and personal information that has been forgotten.

Remotivation was originated by Mrs. Dorothy Hoskins Smith in 1956 at the Philadelphia State Hospital. One of the earliest Reality Orientation programs, the Aide Centered Activity Program for Elderly Patients, was initiated in 1958 at Winter Veterans Administration Hospital, Topeka, Kansas. In 1961 a similar program was established at the Mental Health Institute, Mount Pleasant, Iowa. In 1965 the Reality Orientation technique was further refined at the Veterans Administration Hospital, Tuscaloosa, Alabama, where training programs currently are offered. Today the rehabilitation techniques of Reality Orientation and Remotivation are used in combination as a therapeutic process.

As a treatment method, Reality Orientation and Remotivation is based on the principle that even the most severely impaired mental patient, including the very old, is capable of improvement when exposed to a consistent, continuously administered therapeutic program. Its primary use is to bring confused and disoriented patients back to reality, especially those whose confusion accompanies accidents, illness, strokes, and old age.

Reality reinforcement is used on a 24-hour basis with patients in Reality Orientation programs and consists of two basic treatments: (1) patients are continually stimulated informally, through repetitive orientation; and (2) patients are placed in a formal or structured group where they meet and compete with other patients, which forces the individual out of isolation and back into the environment.

Reality Orientation is a simple technique which, ideally, begins in the home or hospital immediately after the first signs of confusion are noted in the patient. Reeducation is started by helping the patient use that part of the cerebral function which has not been damaged through accident or injury. Basic information (name, date, month, year, time) is constantly repeated to the patient until it is retained and accepted as fact. To supplement hourly and daily reorientation on the wards and dayrooms of a nursing home or hospital, the patient is taken to a special class in Reality Orientation. Classes, which meet for 30 minutes daily, vary in size from two to eight, and are taught by trained specialists. During these classes, the patient is given additional basic information and is helped to relearn it by associating words with pictures and objects.

The class instructor repeatedly presents current and personal information to each patient. When such basic information as name, date, month, and year has been relearned, the instructor presents other information to the patient, such as that person's age, hometown, and former occupation. The teaching process is individualized and related to each patient's degree of present confusion, former level of education, and physiological and psychological readiness for learning. New learning tasks are introduced only when prior levels have been thoroughly mastered. In addition, the instructor never increases the patients' frustrations by asking them to remember some things that they have forgotten. Each correct response is rewarded with verbal praise.

Successful Reality Orientation is usually accompanied by the patient's renewed interest in personal grooming and eating habits. The patient may appear happier in the immediate environment and in the presence of visitors. The person may even ask to participate in other group programs and activities offered in the rehabilitation facility.

Materials used in Reality Orientation classes can include any brightly colored pictures related to the reality topics being presented, such as large calendars, large-faced clocks, maps, and other items. A Reality Orientation board is used in the class (and for bedfast patients) to list the current year, month, day of the week, menu for the next meal, weather, and other pertinent facts. Because many elderly patients have visual and hearing problems, all written information should be in large print and all verbal instructions should be spoken slowly, distinctly, and directly to the person being addressed. If an instructor keeps talking to the patient as though a correct answer is expected, the patient may be able to give it, especially if not allowed to retreat into a confused state. Patients should be encouraged to develop hobbies, read newspapers, watch current events on television, and take part in other scheduled activities and programs.

Attitude therapy is considered an integral part of Reality Orientation and is employed to establish and maintain a consistent staff attitude toward each patient. According to Folsom (1966, p. 57) these attitudes include the following:

1. The attitude of *kind firmness* used with depressed or otherwise uncooperative patients who must be gently coerced into action.
2. The attitude of *active friendliness* used with the withdrawn, apathetic patient whose muteness and unkempt appearance announce to the world the person's profound sense of helplessness and failure. This patient must be loved back to health, and the staff must make constant overtures to keep a spark of response alive.
3. The attitude of *passive friendliness* is used with those patients who are fearful and suspicious of others and constantly on guard against them. Such patients are easily overwhelmed by others and withdraw even from kindness. Assistance cannot be pressed upon them but must be available whenever they need it.
4. The *matter of fact* attitude is applied to demanding, querulous patients who must eventually learn to take the responsibility for their own behavior.
5. The *no demand* attitude for the angry, frantic patient who has been robbed of his or her defenses and who is unable to control internal destructive impulses. Such patients are permitted ventilation and even acting out of their anger, providing they do not harm themselves or others. No demands are made of them, but the solicitous presence of the attendant and other staff members makes them aware of the help and support that is available to them when they are ready to accept it.

Attitude therapy makes it possible for a patient's personal requirements to be met with a degree of consistency that encourages the abandonment of self-defeating behaviors and the learning of new and effective ways of coping with the environment.

After patients have completed the basic and advanced reality orientation classes, and if they are beginning to come out of their confusion, they are graduated to a Remotivation group of 8 to 10 patients. Remotivation is a technique of simple group therapy used with semiconfused or regressed patients. Generally the group meets for approximately an hour at a time, once or twice a week. Remotivation usually is conducted in five steps and includes discussions designed to lead the patient from the past into the present, with projections into the future. Personal and societal awareness are prime targets of Remotivation. This is the final treatment phase before discharge.

The combining of the techniques of Reality Orientation and Remotivation appears to be somewhat successful in the treatment of nursing-home and hospitalized geriatric patients. According to the Veterans Administration in Tuscaloosa, Alabama (1966, p. 7), after a four-year program of Reality Orientation and Remotivation involving 227 patients, 20 percent were discharged to their homes and families, 49 percent remained hospitalized, 10 percent had discharge plans, and the remaining 21 percent were still in Reality Orientation and Remotivation or were transferred to other intensive-care facilities.

SENSORY TRAINING

Sensory Training is a structured, sequential process which can be an individual or shared group experience. As a rehabilitation tool, Sensory Training was developed during the early 1960s for use with children with perceptual-motor impairments. Since then it has been adapted for use with regressed and disoriented psychiatric patients and residents of nursing homes suffering from chronic brain syndrome who are regressed, blind, or wheelchair-bound and do not participate in the organized activity program. In nursing homes the basic emphasis in Sensory Training is to rehabilitate function or prevent further deterioration of regressed geriatric patients by providing various types of stimuli that arouse the patient's senses and promote awareness and meaningful responses.

The basic elements of a Sensory Training program include the following:
1. Differentiated stimuli to improve perception and response to the environment.
2. Stimulation of all sensory receptors.
    a. Auditory stimulation—planned social-group communication, recognition of planned musical-appreciation stimulation, recognition and discrimination of planned and programmed taped sounds (home, street, every-day sounds).
    b. Olfactory stimulation—the presentation of substances or materials with distinct odors, such as perfume, garlic, and lemon, so that the patients can identify and differentiate between the various scents.
    c. Tactile stimulation—recognition and discrimination of textures such as wood, sandpaper, cotton, and sponge. Touching, feeling, and rubbing the objects for identification should be encouraged.

    d.   Visual stimulation—recognition and discrimination of colors and shapes.
    e.   Gustatory stimulation—tasting sweet, sour, spicy, or salty food for recognition and discrimination.
    f.   Kinesthetic and proprioceptive stimulation—planned motor activities to develop an awareness of the movement of various parts of the body, including the identification of the body part being moved.
3. Specifically ordered, structured activities designed to increase sensitivity to stimuli by the individual patient's discrimination and response. The group interaction setting is especially beneficial for producing a response-feedback effect in the patient.
4. Program goals designed to do the following.
    a.   Stimulate the patient's awareness of self and others.
    b.   Orient the patient to reality.
    c.   Increase the patient's alertness to environmental stimuli.
    d.   Improve the patient's level of functioning in the areas of concentration, tolerance, judgment, and manual dexterity.

In most settings, Sensory Training groups are small and consist of four to seven patients and a leader who are seated in a closed circle. All members of the group usually wear name tags. Sessions begin with introductions that include such tactile contacts as hand touching, hand holding, or hand shaking. The purpose of the training is then explained to the group. This is followed by orientation of the group members to such basic facts as the time, place, and date. Next, a series of sensory stimulation exercises is introduced.

Sensory Training sessions meet for approximately 30 to 60 minutes daily, or less frequently, depending on the needs of the group. During the entire session the patients are bombarded with sensory stimuli and suggestions and non-threatening opportunities for social interaction. Most sessions end with a group activity such as singing a simple song.

Agencies using Sensory Training usually have on-site seminars for staff-training purposes.

HORTICULTURE THERAPY

The National Council for Therapy and Rehabilitation through Horticulture was created in 1973 to promote the use of flowers and plants as therapy for the physically and mentally handicapped.

Having patients tend flowers and plants is not a new idea. In 1768 Benjamin Rush maintained that digging in the soil could cure the mentally ill; in 1806 Spanish hospitals used gardening to help mental patients; and, in the early nineteenth century, a Dr. Gregory in North Scotland claimed he could cure insanity by compelling patients to do farm work. Modern horticultural therapists do not make such sweeping claims, but they do point out that flowers and plants seem to be good medicine for victims of strokes, accidents, Parkinson's disease, and mental retardation.

Frequently, horticulture programs let patients perform useful, interesting tasks for the first time in their lives, tasks which do not require routine, mechanical ability. For the nursing-home patient, tending plants is a reason for getting out of bed, a motivation that many such patients need, and a therapy that works because they know that the greenery depends on them for growth and life.

Horticulture Therapy is based on the belief that disabilities can be transformed into abilities when handicapped persons have the opportunity to work with plants—flowers, vegetables, shrubs, and trees. The objective of this international organization is to open doors for the use of these horticultural skills in employment and recreation.

Horticulture Therapy has been used successfully to remotivate emotionally disturbed, severely regressed adults; tough psychological criminals; blind; and mentally retarded patients, many of whom have been able to secure successful employment as a result of their new skills. One 70-year-old graduate of such a program built a greenhouse in her backyard to sell bedding plants and dish gardens to supplement her Social Security income.

Additional information on this new form of therapy and rehabilitation can be obtained by writing the National Council for Therapy and Rehabilitation through Horticulture, Mount Vernon, Virginia 22121.

MUSIC THERAPY

The rehabilitation technique of Music Therapy uses music scientifically and functionally as the tool for producing desirable behavioral and attitudinal changes in the human organism. The music therapist sets attainable, definable goals and structures the therapeutic environment to insure that the patient lengthens his temporal commitment to desirably elicited behaviors. Becoming a polished musician is not the ultimate goal of Music Therapy. Its value, especially with psychiatric patients, is its potential for producing varying degrees of positive physical, mental, emotional, and social responses in the patient.

Music Therapy utilizes three basic processes. The first process is inherent in the music itself. Music is a structured, real event that takes place in time, stimulates the aural sense, and demands a discriminative response from the individual. Activities used in a therapeutic situation include singing, creative movement and dance, playing instruments, and listening to music. This broad spectrum of activities makes music easily adaptable to the individual's own physical, intellectual, and emotional level of development.

The second basic process in Music Therapy is that of self-organization. Music provides a means of self-expression, allowing the individual to communicate his moods, feelings for others, and attitudes about his life on a nonverbal level. Activities can be structured to offer socially acceptable ways to express negative feelings or to allow for tension release. Success is built in because activities can be as simple as playing a phonograph or as complex as directing an orchestra. Such success-oriented experiences allow for increased self-esteem in the patient.

The third Music-Therapy process deals with interpersonal relationships and social interactions. As a nonverbal form of communication, group-music activity requires cooperation from all members of the group. Each and every participant must learn to develop realistic and socially acceptable personal-behavior patterns and social skills and then to accept full responsibility for his or her actions within the group. If movement is combined with music, the additional element of acceptable physical contact with others is added to the therapeutic environment. Because music can be used as entertainment or recreation, its use as therapy has carry-over value into normal life patterns.

Frequently, the patient who responds to no other medium can be reached through music. The nonthreatening environment, scope, and infinite variety offered by musical experiences permit the patient to elicit basic human responses without fear of censure. Music, as a nonverbal form of communication, also permits the free expression of deeply seated personal emotions and feelings.

Through participation in group-music activities, such as bands, orchestras, and choruses, the withdrawn or hyperactive patient can learn the emotional control and social adjustment necessary for resocialization back into the community. Such group activities teach the patient to conform to the rules of group behavior and develop within the patient a sense of belonging, self-respect, and accomplishment.

Music Therapy can help to improve the patient's personal music skills. In addition, a deep appreciation for music can be developed just by listening to music. Thus, music and music-related activity can be enjoyed in the pursuit of leisure-time activities.

Many colleges and universities with large music departments offer specialized training leading to a degree in Music Therapy. Additional information can be obtained from the National Association for Music Therapy Incorporated, Box 610, Lawrence, Kansas 66044.

MOVEMENT (DANCE) THERAPY

Movement Therapy is the psychotherapeutic use of movement as a process which furthers the emotional and physical integration of the individual. The term Movement Therapy is preferable to Dance Therapy (Weisbrod 1972, p. 66) primarily because it is less threatening to the individual and is a natural or fundamental dimension of human behavior.

As a nonverbal form of self-expression, Movement Therapy can be adapted for use with any group. A good therapist will utilize appropriate aspects of movement, dance, and sensory stimulation in all planned therapy sessions. The broad goals of Movement Therapy include the following: release of tension (relaxation); reduction of anxiety; emotional release through safe, structured, rhythmic action; resocialization through group interaction and shared movement experiences; improvement of body image, a sense of self-worth, and self-confidence in one's own body actions; stimulation of verbalization; and physical conditioning and exercise.

In geriatric Movement Therapy the goals are usually based on the physiological, psychological, and sociological needs and desires of the individual and the group. (See chapter 2, Biological/Physiological Aspects of Aging; chapter 3, Psychological Aspects of Aging; and chapter 4, Sociological Aspects of Aging.)

Movement-Therapy sessions can be directed or nondirected. During the initial stages of therapy it may be necessary for the therapist to use directed movement to motivate the patient and set the framework for the therapeutic encounter. Any directed movement should proceed logically and be based on the mood, movement capacity, and the social level of the individual or group. Music can be an extremely helpful facilitator in this regard, especially to create the desired mood and involvement of the participants, to lend rhythmic support, and to direct the patients with their own movements. In nondirected movement the patient should lead the mood and take the session wherever it goes. In all therapy sessions the skilled therapist will encourage the patient by lending support and understanding through movement. This can be done if the therapist picks up, exaggerates, and responds through movement to the patient's movements and emotional expressions. Such procedures are extremely useful in establishing a desirable therapeutic patient/therapist relationship. In addition, through movement and music, the skilled therapist will be able to meet the patient at that person's level by picking up behavior cues from the patient. By manipulating the environment, the therapist can help the patient work through his or her problems in movement.

Movement Therapy is especially useful with those patients where language is a barrier rather than a bridge to communication. Movement is relatively nonthreatening; it helps the patient feel more comfortable and less threatened by others and provides a socially acceptable environment for working out conflicts, fantasies, hostilities, and aggressions.

Group Movement Therapy can be extremely useful in helping the patient develop an understanding of "self" as an individual and a member of the group.

In addition, an awareness and respect for other individuals in the group can be fostered. No expected level of performance or behavior is required in Movement Therapy. The only unacceptable movements are those which may hurt the individual or someone else in the group. A skillful therapist will help the patient with destructive tendencies to symbolically and appropriately work through these behaviors in movement. Percussive instruments, such as drums, can be especially helpful with those patients expressing destruction, aggression, or hostility.

The circle formation is particularly useful in reducing anxiety, fostering a sense of cohesiveness, lending support to the patient, and fostering movement expression without the overwhelming fear of rejection. Movement Therapy also permits the externalization of feelings about "self" without having to relate to a specific person, which may produce anxiety.

The primary objective of Movement Therapy is to help patients feel more comfortable within themselves by completely expressing "self" through movement—by experiencing strong emotions, thus cleansing "self" of these feelings and developing a sense of freedom and newness. This can only occur if the therapeutic environment is one of acceptance and trust. Movement Therapy should help patients to relax and release body tensions, to realize that they are not alone and that there are others with similar problems, and to develop within themselves the freedom to make choices. This development of freedom of the body through movement is especially important as a carry-over into the freedom to direct one's own life. The therapeutic involvement should help the patient attain a more positive self-image by sensitizing "self" to the body, improving physical coordination, increasing freedom of movement, and releasing pent-up emotions. It also teaches the patient to work out aggressions and hostilities, to deal better with "self" and others, to develop social awareness, and to experience social and personal success.

Because inactivity, a developed habit for many older persons, is difficult to overcome, motivation for activity is essential, especially in geriatric Movement Therapy. The motivation techniques must be geared toward bringing to the mature adult pleasurable experiences, which are designed to fulfill basic instinctual needs. This can be accomplished in directed Movement Therapy if the therapist utilizes the following activity guidelines when adapting the movement experiences to the unique needs and limitations of each and every individual in the group.

1. Give encouragement and reinforcement frequently.
2. Keep all movement within the physical tolerance level of the individual. Avoid movements that may cause pain, strain, or other physical discomfort. This may necessitate a modification of activity, or the creation of special movement combinations and sequences for each individual or special group.

3. Because most mature adults know their own physical limitations, permit individual modification of activity, especially regarding velocity and range of motion.
4. Recognize subtle cues of fatigue, stress, impatience, disinterest, difficulty and pain, and change the activity accordingly. Promote evidence of interest, pleasure or interaction, and responses of the individual and the group.
5. Bypass the sensory losses of the individual by using a multisensory approach. Supplement sensory stimulation through existing, less impaired sensory modalities. Combine auditory, visual, tactile, gustatory, and kinesthetic cues whenever possible. Although the key modalities used in a Movement-Therapy program are tactile and kinesthetic, these should always be supplemented with auditory (therapist's voice) and visual (therapist's demonstration) cues.
6. Plan movement experiences to guarantee the individual's need for security and physiological and psychological safety.
7. Create a congenial, supportive environment which stimulates group laughter, relaxation, and exhilaration. Avoid any reference to fatigue and depression.
8. Create a feeling of group consciousness and develop a helping relationship among the participants. Help everyone achieve a feeling of belonging to the group.
9. Accept every adult's limitations and accommodate all activity to those limitations. This will help to create an atmosphere that facilitates the recognition of each individual's unique achievements.
10. Stimulate the neuromuscular mechanism by including active and passive relaxation in each therapy session.

The movement techniques and sequences included in a Movement-Therapy program should permit each mature adult to use all body joints to their maximum range of flexion, extension, and rotation. In addition, contraction and relaxation of all major muscle groups should be included. This can be done isometrically, isotonically, or in combination. The force of gravity should also be incorporated into the lessons.

Geriatric Movement Therapy can be performed from a sitting position in a straight-back chair or a wheelchair. Some activities can be performed while standing if they are within the tolerance level of the individual. Activities, such as arm swings, can be performed in a circle while everyone is sitting and holding hands. When this technique is used, care should be taken to insure that the severely involved individual is not forced to move beyond his or her range of pain tolerance.

The movement therapist working in geriatrics should be qualified as a Movement (Dance) Therapist and have a background in gerontology. Many schools across the country currently offer certification programs in these two areas.

ART THERAPY

Art Therapy as a form of psychotherapy is based on the recognition that humanity's fundamental thoughts and feelings are derived from the unconscious, often reaching expression in images rather than words. The psychoanalytic approach to the mechanisms of repression, projection, identification, sublimation, and condensation are accepted as basic to the treatment methods of Art Therapy.

The dynamics of Art Therapy are many. Symbolic communication between the therapist and patient is encouraged by means of pictorial projection. A patient in Art Therapy draws spontaneous, unconscious projections of his deep-seated emotions, feelings, fears, and frustrations. He is encouraged to paint what he sees within himself rather than what he sees before himself. The therapist encourages the patient to give free associations to the images that are being made and does not interpret the subject's drawings but, rather, encourages the patient to assume an active role in explaining his own creations. The process of discovering the meaning of the symbolic art takes place within the framework of the established transference to the therapist. If the patient is unable to verbalize the meaning of the drawings, the therapist inquires about the mood in which the drawings were created or the order in which the colors were used. The therapist's questioning may enable the creator to interpret the symbolic significance of the picture.

Frequently the scribble technique is used to help the patient liberate spontaneous expression. The patient draws on large sheets of paper with pastels or poster paints and is encouraged to draw without conscious planning by making a continuous flowing line on the paper. Next, the patient is asked to look at the scribble pattern and try to discover some suggestion of a design, an object, or a person. Scribble drawings are of value to Art Therapy as a means of encouraging free associations.

Art Therapy can be employed in individual or group situations. When used with a group, Art Therapy has been effective by drawing murals on large sheets of paper and then having the group express free associations to the art production.

Art Therapy places emphasis on an active, interpersonal relationship between the patient and the therapist. The art therapist encourages the patient to develop free associations to the pictures, whether they express dreams, fantasies, or wishes. The activities of persons in Art Therapy, therefore, consist of expression through spontaneous pictures and verbal communication with the therapist, centering around the individual's conflicts and problems, which may or may not have been expressed in the drawn pictures.

The transference relationship is significant in Art Therapy. The patient is convinced that whatever is expressed by the paintings is accepted by the therapist.

Thus, the patient's art productions are treated as a mirror that reflects the individual's motives.

Through the nonverbal media of painting, drawing, etching, and related art forms, and with the help of a therapist, patients can begin to better understand themselves and their problems so that the long process of behavior change to more socially acceptable forms can take place.

For many older individuals, art in its pure form can be therapeutic in and of itself because of the many hours of free time it can fill. This is especially true after the individual has discovered the joy of working with the various art forms.

Many college and university art departments offer work leading to a specialization in Art Therapy. Frequently Music, Dance, and Art Therapy are combined when working with the psychiatric patient in hospitals or institutions.

RECREATION AS THERAPY

According to the National Therapeutic Recreation Society, Therapeutic Recreation is a special service within the broad area of recreation services. It is a process that utilizes recreation services for purposive intervention in some physical, emotional, or social behavior to bring about a desired change in that behavior and to promote the growth and development of the individual (AAHPER/BEH 1973, p. 5).

In hospitals and special institutions recreation services should be provided as part of the social continuum. Frequently the patient needs an opportunity for recreation as pure recreation without the fear of being booby-trapped into a clinically significant admission. Such recreation is therapeutic in the sense that it is a means of increasing the effectiveness of other therapies; while not curative in itself, recreation helps create the milieu for successful patient treatment.

Recreation is a way of helping patients direct their attention away from their illnesses toward something enjoyable. Thus, they become a little happier, a little more confident, a little more refreshed. Recreation can motivate and reawaken in the patient an interest in things that are fun and encourage the healing process by promoting early ambulation and creating an immediate incentive for activity.

According to Paul Haun (1965, p. 56),

> In essence, recreation services help to create in the patient a desirable psychological state by contributing to his self-confidence, his optimism, and his ability to accept the inevitable discomfort of his illness. It combats the fears, the isolation, and the resistances that threaten recovery. It may, particularly in chronic illnesses, contribute importantly to motivation. In a physical sense, it promotes the return of function, helps the patient compensate for transient as well as

permanent defects, assists in the restoration of normal metabolic processes, acts as an effective physiologic tonic, and, in general, shortens
convalescence. It can, I believe, be effectively used in hospitals of every
kind and with patients of every age.

In his text, Recreation: A Medical Viewpoint (p. 70), Dr. Haun has outlined
the following indices by which recreation services to patients can be measured
purely in terms of effectiveness as recreation.
1. Increased number of patients attending
2. Increased patient responsiveness as observers or participants
3. Increased identification with group in team games
4. Higher level of sportsmanship in competitive games
5. Greater facility and improved quality of performance in individual recreational pursuits
6. Increased number of patients seeking instruction in performance skills
7. Movement of static patient population from simpler to more complex
   recreative activities
8. More frequent expression of preference and choice by the patient

In summary, recreation activities included in hospitals and special institutions can be therapeutic, recreational, or both. The skilled recreation therapist
can incorporate both aspects into the programming. Currently, many colleges
and universities offer certification programs in Therapeutic Recreation.

Numerous other forms of psychotherapy are used alone or in various combinations to comprise the total therapeutic milieu in hospitals and special institutions for the mature adult. The scope of this book does not permit the
inclusion of all of these various methods. The interested reader should refer to
the following list of selected references for additional information.

SELECTED REFERENCES

American Alliance for Health, Physical Education, and Recreation and the
    Bureau of Education for the Handicapped. Guidelines for professional
    preparation programs for personnel involved in physical education and
    recreation for the handicapped. Washington, D.C.: American Alliance for
    Health, Physical Education, and Recreation, 1973.
Chown, Sheila M., ed. Human aging. Harmondsworth, England: Penguin Books, 1961.
Cohen, Irene, and Segall, Jeannie. Using dance therapy in the extended care
    facility. Nursing Homes, December-January 1974, 28-30.
Cumming, Elaine, and Henry, W. E. Growing old. New York: Basic Books, 1961.
Folsom, James C. Reality orientation for the elderly mental patient. Journal of
    Geriatric Psychiatry, 1968, 1, 291-307.

aston, E. Thayer. *Music in therapy.* New York: Macmillan, 1968.

insburg, Isajah. Therapeutic recreation: A modality for rehabilitation of the aged. *Therapeutic Recreation Journal,* 1974, *VIII (1),* 42-46.

adin, Catherine B. Reality orientation and remotivation in health care facilities. *Expanding Horizons in Therapeutic Recreation II.* University of Illinois: Office of Recreation and Park Resources, 1974, 111-115.

asser, William. *Reality therapy: A new approach to psychiatry.* New York: Harper & Row, 1975.

ordon, Chad. Sociological aspects of aging. *Time,* August 3, 1970, 23.

un, Paul. *Recreation: A medical viewpoint.* New York: Bureau of Publications, Teachers College, Columbia University, 1965.

avinghurst, R. J. Flexibility and the social roles of the retirees. *American Journal of Sociology,* 1954, *LIX,* 249-260.

inlen, Francis W.; Degaard, John G.; Barrell, Robert P.; and Wolfe, Alan S. Recreation therapy research with geriatric patients: History of a cooperative project. *Therapeutic Recreation Journal,* vol. 3, 1, 1969, 35-37.

aus, Richard. *Therapeutic recreation service: Principles and practice.* Philadelphia: W. B. Saunders, 1973.

ether, Herman J. *Problems of aging.* Encino, Calif.: Dickenson Publishing, 1967.

ason, Kathleen C., ed. *Dance therapy: Focus on dance VII.* Washington, D.C.: American Alliance for Health, Physical Education, and Recreation, 1974.

itchell, Robert A. Reality orientation for brain damaged patients. *Staff,* 1966, *3,* 3-4.

aumburg, Margaret. *Dynamically oriented art therapy: Its principles and practice.* New York: Grune & Stratton, 1966.

chmais, Claire. What is dance therapy? *Journal of Health, Physical Education, and Recreation,* January 1976, 39.

aapiro, Alex. A pilot program in music therapy with residents of a home for the aged. *Gerontologist,* vol. 9, no. 2, 1969, 128-133.

human, Bonnie. Dance therapy for the emotionally disturbed. *Journal of Health, Physical Education, and Recreation,* September 1973, 61-62.

aulbee, Lucille. Nursing intervention for confusion of the elderly. *Alabama Nurse,* 1968, *22,* 1-3.

aulbee, Lucille R., and Folsom, James C. Reality orientation for geriatric patients. *Hospital and Community Psychiatry,* 1966, *17,* 133-135.

eterans Administration. Pilot program to reorient and rehabilitate older mental patients achieve good results. *Geriatric Focus,* 1966, *5,* 7.

eisbrod, J. A. Shaping a body image through movement therapy. *Music Education,* 1972, *58,* 66-69.

asgur, Steven S. The senior olympics: Games for adults who won't quit. *Geriatrics,* vol. 30, 1, January 1975, 120-125.

6
SPORTS AND EXERCISE

Youth, large, lusty, loving—
Youth, full of grace, force, fascination,
Do you know that Old Age may come after you,
With equal grace, force, fascination?
—Walt Whitman

Many mature adults are relatively young and fit and possess a reasonable degree of skill in a variety of sports. Unless contraindicated, these individuals can participate in most active sports, exercise, and physical conditioning programs with few, if any, modifications. This is especially true for those individuals who have attained and maintained a reasonable degree of physical fitness throughout their life span. The individual who has been sedentary most of his or her adult life may need to modify activity or begin with only short periods of participation in vigorous sports, gradually increasing the intensity and duration of participation as endurance improves.

Regardless of the level of fitness at which a mature adult enters a recreation program, or the guidelines provided by the physician, if signs of fatigue or breathlessness occur, activity should cease immediately. Such individuals should be requested to visit their physician for reevaluation regarding exercise limits.

Before enrolling participants in sports and exercise programs, medical clearance is highly recommended as a medical safeguard for the participant and as a program guide for the activity program director. Information should include any medical problems that may limit vigorous activity or require the modification of specific sports and exercises to meet the physical-exercise needs of the individual.

SAMPLE

Medical Clearance Form

Name:_____Physician:_____

Address:_____

Phone:_____ Date of birth: _____

Date of medical examination:_____

The above named individual has been examined and is physically fit to participate in the following activities (please check those that are appropriate):

____ Swimming   ____ Vigorous fitness activities

____ Golf   ____ Moderate fitness activities

____ Tennis   ____ Mild fitness activities

____ Skiing   ____ Hiking

____ Ice skating   ____ Badminton

____ (Other—depending on
      program offerings)

The following activity limitations should be observed:_____
_____

Special problems which may necessitate caution: _____
_____

Special activities are needed to develop the following weaknesses:_____
_____

Other pertinent information:_____
_____

   With proper modification, most mature adults can participate in and enjoy
a variety of active sports and moderate to vigorous exercise programs. Such activities can be stimulating and enjoyable and will provide the participant with
desirable psychological, physiological, and sociological benefits. The activities
selected for inclusion in this chapter are frequently chosen by mature adults as
enjoyable leisure activities. Rather than including detailed skill descriptions,
which can be found in most physical-education and recreation textbooks, skill

modifications and special teaching techniques that may be appropriate to use for a majority of mature adults are included.

SWIMMING

Swimming is one of the most popular active sports enjoyed by mature adults and one of the best for the handicapped mature adult. Not only does swimming involve all of the major muscle groups in the human organism, but it can be adjusted easily to provide the participant with mild, moderate, or strenuous activity. Progressive conditioning can be achieved in swimming if the distance to be swum is gradually increased.

Age itself is relatively unimportant as a barrier in learning to swim later in life. Of greater significance is the mature adult's level of motivation, basic motor capacity, energy level, and previous motor experiences. Once a good student/ teacher rapport has been established, and with proper guidance, most mature adults can learn to swim or improve their swimming proficiency. The time required for the older beginner to learn, however, is greater than that required for the average college-age student.

The acceptable techniques of instructing any beginning swimmer, including orientation to the water, basic water adjustment, breathing, breath holding, rhythmic breathing, bobbing, back and prone floats and recoveries, back and prone glides and kick glides, changing positions, changing directions, leveling off from a jump or dive, treading water, and combined swimming strokes on the front, back, and side should be included in the instructional phase of the program (Moran and Kalakian 1977, p. 337). It is extremely important that the teacher progress slowly, especially at the beginning stages of learning, so that all fears are alleviated. Fear can be extremely harmful to the aging organism because it is usually accompanied by increased heart action, increased respiration, and rapid fatigue, all of which cause undue stress to the cardiorespiratory system.

Basic skill and stroke modifications may be necessary for some swimmers. If, for example, the mature adult is overweight and in poor physical condition, standing from a back float may be difficult. When this problem occurs, teach the swimmer to roll from the back to the face and then assume a standing position. Technique modifications also may be necessary for the individual with severe arthritis who, because of pain, may have difficulty with the full range of joint-motion activity or activities involving the use of specific joints. Care should be taken with these individuals to avoid undue pain, which may occur if joint motions are not properly modified. Begin with underwater recoveries and increase the range of the stroke motion only when it is not contraindicated. A slow, easy flutter kick with an underwater arm recovery (human stroke) is recommended in the face position. The finning stroke is recommended in the back position. When the finning stroke is mastered, the arm movements can be changed to those of the elementary backstroke. In most cases, the breaststroke kick should be avoided for individuals with knee problems. If the scissor kick is difficult to perform, a flutter kick may be substituted in the sidestroke. Water of at least 87 ° is recommended for the arthritic.

The amount of detailed skill analysis, the explanation used, and the degree of mastery anticipated for the swimmer must be adapted to the needs of each individual and group. Most mature adults are more interested in learning general techniques, rather than the fine and detailed aspects, of various swimming strokes. Therefore, form should not be stressed.

Because many mature adults may suffer from varying degrees of visual and auditory losses, which are intensified when hearing aides and eye glasses are removed before entering the water, a multisensory teaching approach should be used whenever possible. The simultaneous utilization of two or more senses reinforces learning and makes it more rapid and permanent. The use of these various sensory modalities should include combinations of the following:

1. Visual stimulation. The eyes are stimulated by good demonstrations and simple visual aids. Demonstrations should be performed as close to the visually impaired as possible, preferably by an instructor in the water, with the students as close as possible. The demonstrator should exaggerate the swimming motions being performed.

2. Auditory stimulation. The ears are stimulated by clear, concise, and accurate word descriptions of the activity to be performed. Explanations should be given as close to the hearing impaired as possible, preferably by an instructor in the water, with the students as close as possible. Avoid lengthy, detailed explanations.

3. Kinesthetic stimulation. The manual manipulation of body parts, or assistive technique, consists of the guidance of body parts through the desired motion. This capitalizes on kinesthetic (proprioceptive) feedback from the muscles to the brain and helps the mature adult feel and sense where his or her body parts are as they move. This technique is extremely effective with mature adults learning to swim. Flotation devices are effective for providing necessary support when patterning some swimming movements.

4. Tactile stimulation. The touching of body parts enables the mature adult to feel the part of the body to be moved, such as an elbow to lift on the front crawl. Tactile stimulation is effective in the reinforcement of visual and auditory stimulation.

Frequently, the trial-and-error practice method with corrections is also effective when teaching swimming to the mature adult. These various teaching techniques can also be applied successfully to the teaching of the various other activities included in this text.

Because many mature adults move slowly, adequate time should be provided for dressing, showering, getting into instructional formations, grasping new ideas, and learning new skills and techniques. The instructor should be patient and not hurry the group. In addition, because some of the swimmers may tire easily, chairs or benches on the pool deck are useful to provide the rest some swimmers may require during the class period.

Berlin (1960, p. 14) made the following observations and recommendations after conducting a beginners' swimming program for mature adults ranging in age from 59 to 79 years, with a mean age of 69.5 years.

1. With regular, twice-a-week swimming practice, mature adults can develop endurance in swimming, ranging from one width of the pool to a 60-minute endurance swim. A 15-minute endurance swim was average for the group.
2. The exercise values of swimming seem to be stimulating and desirable to the participants. These values were reported by the group to include: immediate physical exhilaration followed by fatigue, a noticeable increase in appetite following the activity, and various claims of relief from arthritis such as lessened stiffness and greater range of joint mobility.
3. If desirable therapeutic effects are to be achieved, the water and air temperatures should be maintained at 85°.
4. False teeth should be removed before swimming.
5. Make flippers and swim boards available and use skill testing as these devices have a motivating effect on the group.
6. Never encourage aging beginners to work beyond their limits or desires; instead, concentrate on building the swimmer's confidence.
7. Limit class size to 20 persons. If possible, divide into smaller groups and classify the learners according to skill level.
8. Plan the class so that at least three instructors are available. One should remain on the deck to survey the entire pool area. The other two should be free to provide the individualized instruction in the water needed by the participants.

WATER EXERCISES

In addition to the fun and exercise traditional swimming provides, water is an excellent medium for performing land exercises because of its special characteristics: (1) the buoyant effect of water on the human organism makes many movements that are difficult or impossible to perform on land relatively easy; and (2) the resistance of water against the body part being moved makes the exercise more beneficial by increasing the workload of the muscles involved.

A water temperature of 87° is recommended for water exercise to stimulate circulation and aid relaxation. Handrails in the water and ropes stretched across the pool are excellent aides for the poorly coordinated. In addition, if the water is shallow, benches can be placed in the water for use by the physically handicapped with very limited leg mobility. Or a pool with stairs at the shallow end can be used for the same purpose.

Water exercises are extremely beneficial in developing muscular strength, improving muscle tone, developing stamina and endurance, enhancing coordination, flexibility, and agility, improving circulation, and developing confidence. Correct body positions and breathing should be emphasized during the exercise sessions. Exercises can range from walking across the pool to using all parts of the body through all ranges of motion, i.e., arm swings, leg swings, knee flexion followed by full extension, and elbow flexion followed by full extension. Bobbing and treading, which stress breathing techniques, are excellent for the experienced swimmer to increase levels of fitness.

CAMPING AND OUTDOOR EDUCATION

Organized day or residential camping and other forms of outdoor education are important components of the total recreation program for the mature adult. Such experiences provide sociological, psychological, and physiological benefits. An opportunity is provided for cooperative living in a camping environment, something frequently needed by the mature adult whose children have left home or whose spouse has died and left a void in the daily living routine. New social relationships can be developed at day or residential camps and in outdoor education experiences to replace those lost through retirement or death. The environment is one of relaxation in which personal tensions, such as those caused by the pressures of daily living, can be forgotten. In addition, a new and different environment is provided for exploration, enjoyment, education, and creativity; thus, the element of fun can be put back into living.

Camping and outdoor education experiences for the mature adult should provide the following:

1. Conditions that foster simple and wholesome living
2. A place for enriching experiences unobtainable in urban areas
3. Opportunities for the development of a wholesome attitude toward self and others, including peer friendships and the enjoyment of shared group experiences
4. An atmosphere for personal growth and continued enjoyable living through active participation in sports, creative arts, social functions, educational lectures, discussion groups, and other activities
5. An inexpensive holiday away from the city and normal routine
6. An opportunity for a sensitive, personal contact with nature that is deeper and more meaningful than just the enjoyment and appreciation of the beauty of nature

7. Opportunities for wholesome fun and pleasurable experiences in an outdoor setting
8. An opportunity to renew old and establish new friendships
9. An opportunity to learn new skills
10. Something fresh and different to talk about after returning home

Although most campsites are appropriate for use by mature adults, the ideal site should have a relatively smooth and level terrain with only slight elevations and should be dry and free of obnoxious insects. If the campsite is located less than 75 to 100 miles from town and has paved and well-drained roads, some campers can drive their personal automobiles to the campsite without the potential hazards created by long periods behind the wheel and poor traveling conditions. Bus service should be provided for those unable or unwilling to drive. Such bus service should have facilities to accommodate the handicapped, such as a hydraulic wheelchair lift. It is highly recommended that all campers ride the bus to day outings, unless the distance is very short.

Frequently, day or residential campsites can be secured for use by the mature-adult population in early June, late August, September, or between other scheduled camp sessions during the summer months. If weather conditions permit, programs can also be scheduled during the winter months. Many Easter Seal camps include the handicapped mature adult in their regular summer schedule. Such camps provide ideal facilities for other groups of mature adults.

The facilities selected for use by this population should provide for the physical health and comfort of the group. The following recommendations will be helpful in the selection of appropriate facilities.

1. Sleeping cabins or dormitories should be weatherproof with a maximum of four beds per room. Depending on the location of the campsite, heat or air conditioning should be provided. If the beds are double-deckers, only the lower bunks should be used unless an agile camper really prefers the upper bunk. There should be a chair for each bed. When appropriate, accessibility to wheelchairs must be considered. Handrails on ramps or stairs are also recommended.

2. If possible, each cabin should have running water. Toilet facilities should be private and preferably under the same roof, although nearby facilities are acceptable if a night-light is left burning. If mature adults confined to wheelchairs are included in the program, toilet facilities should be easily accessible to wheelchairs. Handrails are desirable. Cleanliness is essential.

3. Living quarters should include comfortable chairs as many mature adults quickly grow weary of hard chairs. Television for rainy days and evening hours, although not absolutely necessary, can provide additional pleasure.

4. The dining-hall chairs and tables should be movable to permit use of the facility for dancing and other activities. Some tables should be of proper height to accommodate wheelchairs.

5. Adequate lighting in all facilities is essential. In addition, shaded night-lights near the floors of the sleeping quarters are desirable, especially for those who may need to use toilet facilities during the night.

Meals can be highlights of a camping program, especially for those campers accustomed to eating alone. The food served should be nourishing, tasty, low in fats, and high in protein and vitamins. Many of the campers will appreciate pre-breakfast and bedtime snacks, as well as mid-morning and mid-afternoon coffee or tea breaks. Meal preparation should give special consideration to individuals with dietary problems. A request for such dietary information should be a part of the camp registration form. When appropriate, special tables can be set up for those individuals with similar dietary problems.

The quality and skill of leadership is the single most important factor for a successful and creative camping or outdoor education experience for the mature adult. As with all camping positions, all job descriptions should be in writing. The staff, both professional and volunteer, should possess the following qualities:

1. A thorough understanding of the physical, mental, emotional, and social potentialities and limitations of the aged. This should include an understanding of the campers' potential physical disabilities, mental deficiencies if the mentally retarded are included in the program, economic problems, and effects of enforced leisure on attitudes.
2. A thorough understanding of the objectives of the camping or outdoor education program.
3. A personality that accepts the camper as an individual, encourages participation in activities, and stimulates the camper's development of a variety of activity interests, skills, and appreciations. Necessary qualities are kindness, patience, understanding, tolerance, personal warmth, and maturity.
4. The ability to tactfully and appropriately assist the handicapped mature adult.

One member of the staff should be a qualified nurse who has professional medical facilities readily accessible. In addition, a physician should be on standby and located not more than 10 to 15 minutes travel time from the campsite. The necessary number and type of other staff and volunteers will depend upon the number of campers served, the degree of the campers' physical or mental limitations, and the kind of activities included in the program. If severely handicapped mature adults are among the campers, a one-to-one camper/volunteer or aide relationship may be needed. Frequently, the nonhandicapped campers enjoy assisting their handicapped campmates.

Because many mature adults are qualified campers, they should be given the opportunity to serve as their own resource specialists for some activities. Many others may want and need the opportunity to assist their campmates who have visual, hearing, or mobility problems. A more successful camping or outdoor education experience will evolve if the campers are actively involved in the total program, including meal preparation, when appropriate. Although some activities should be planned, scheduled, and organized, the major planning and execution of the program should be done with and by the campers, with as few rules and regulations imposed on activity, rest, and relaxation as possible. If this freedom is allowed, the campers will regulate activity and rest to meet their personal physiological, psychological, and sociological needs.

If the weather is extremely warm, vigorous activities should be scheduled early or late in the day. Active and passive activities, suitable for both sexes having various skill-participation levels, should be included. Several activities should be scheduled simultaneously to permit the camper the opportunity to select those activities which will best meet that person's own needs. In addition, activities should consider the individual's personal safety. The following list of activities might be appropriately modified to permit everyone to participate within their physical tolerance level.

Aquatics—fishing, boating, swimming

Art—painting, sculpting

Bicycling

Bird watching

Campfires

Cards

Charades

Cookouts

Crafts—nature crafts, wood carving, lapidary, whittling, basket making, spinning, weaving, crafts that are creative, useful, and inexpensive to permit carry-over back into the community

Creative dramatics

Dancing—folk, square, social

Folk singing

Food-related activities—planting, gardening, harvesting, preserving

Intellectual (cognitive) activities—group discussions on any topics selected by the campers

Music—instrument bands

Nature hikes—special trails set up for wheelchairs, those with very poor eyesight, or limited mobility; walks for pure exercise

Party games

Photography

Physical fitness activities

Range activities—archery, rifle/shotgun shooting and hunting, where appropria

Special events—tours of nearby historical sites, antique hunting

Sports and games—bowling on grass, croquet, golf, tennis, checkers, chess, horseshoes, pool, shuffleboard; choice limited only by available facilities and equipment

Story telling

ALPINE AND NORDIC SKIING

On any typical winter day at many ski areas across the country, one can see several old-timers enjoying both Alpine (downhill) and Nordic (cross-country) skiing. They may ski at a slower pace than in their youth, but the fun is still present. In fact, one Nordic skier from Park City, Utah, is still skiing daily at age 101. Many older (66 years and up) skiers participate annually in Sweden's cross-country ski races. In 1975 Guido Tonella, age 73, finished with a time of 4:45.00 for 42 kilometers. The oldest participant was Jules Furrer, age 79. There is a retired 65-year-old Alpine ski instructor from A Basin, Colorado, who is skiing with two artificial hips, and a 75-year-old retiree at Sun Valley, Idaho, with one artificial hip. Both of these gentlemen are "skiing better than ever." Modern skiing equipment includes specially designed poles with miniature skis on the ends for the one-legged skier. The blind or partially sighted mature adult can learn to ski by following skiers with bells on their poles. The sound of the bells acts as a cue for turning. The hearing impaired with no balance problems will have little difficulty learning to ski. These individuals should, however, inform their instructor of this hearing loss.

Alf Engen, "the Old Man of the Mountain" and a 68-year-old ski-school director at Alta, Utah, can still outski most of his ski instructors. From November through April he spends at least four hours a day on the mountain. According to Alf (Rand 1974, p. 23),

> *More and more people will ski in their later years now. We are all concerned with health. We don't want to sit by the fire. You can start skiing later in life now. Some weekends we get a thousand pupils at Alta, but we never have a batch that does not include people in their sixties.*

Alf gives the following tips to older skiers:

1. Blow like an elk. Some people concentrate so hard that they hold their breath when they ski. Breathe out deliberately and strongly. It makes you relax.
2. Count out loud to yourself. Keep up your rhythm after you plant your pole.
3. Stem your ski. It is no sin to use the learning skier's device of poking one ski out sideways instead of trying to balance on two close-together parallel skis.

4. Turn your skis all the different ways. Don't tackle all the problems with one technique.
5. Press into your boot tops. It makes you keep your knees bent.
6. Sleep low. After skiing at high altitudes all day, recuperate by sleeping as close to sea level as you can. If you are coming to Alta, try spending the first night down in Salt Lake City.
7. Enjoy yourself. Skiing is a game you play for pleasure.

It is recommended that the mature adult who is interested in either Nordic or Alpine skiing take lessons from a certified instructor. Such instructions at many ski schools also include special classes for the partially sighted or one-leg amputee. In most cases the older beginner prefers Nordic to Alpine skiing because of the reduced fear of falling and lower costs. It is interesting to note that Alta, Utah, has given free lifetime ski passes to many of its old timers who have skied at Alta throughout their lives.

SLEIGH RIDES

Sleigh rides can provide enjoyable group winter activity for mature adults. In snow country, sleighs can be hired for such a purpose. Group singing during the sleigh ride is frequently enjoyed by the group. An evening can be made of a sleigh ride if there are refreshments at the conclusion of the ride. This is especially enjoyable if a fireside is available. Even the most severely handicapped mature adult, including the mentally retarded or cerebral palsied, can enjoy a sleigh ride if proper clothing is worn, blankets are provided, and assistance in and out of the sleigh is available.

ICE SKATING

Ice skating is a winter sport that can be enjoyed by most mature adults. Music is very useful in the development of skating rhythm, especially if the skater is apprehensive. An indoor ice-skating rink is preferable for the beginner, but the availability of only outdoor facilities should not deter the inclusion of ice skating in the recreation program. Holding hands is an excellent teaching technique for the beginner or partially sighted skater. This technique lends support to the apprehensive beginner, aids in the development of a proper rhythm, and provides security to the partially sighted. As with other sports, ice skating is not difficult for the mature adult with a hearing loss unless balance is a problem. The degree of hip or knee involvement of an arthritic will be the determining factor in ice-skating ability. Many arthritics may find the cold weather undesirable. If this problem occurs, indoor activities should be programmed.

As with other winter sports, proper clothing is essential when ice skating. Fewer clothes are needed indoors than outdoors, but in most cases the mature adult will feel more comfortable if head and hand clothing are part of the attire. In addition, proper socks to provide warmth and properly fitting ice skates are essential. Many indoor ice-skating rinks provide rental skates at a nominal fee. Indoor rinks also provide instruction for the beginner. Many such facilities will give a group of mature adults special prices if the facilities are used during off hours.

SNOWSHOEING

Snowshoeing is thought to have originated over 4000 years ago in Central Asia and was brought to the Americas by way of the Bering Straits. At the turn of the century snowshoeing was a popular winter sport in New England. Today, primarily because of its low cost, it is becoming increasingly popular for all age groups in snow country across the United States.

As a recreational activity, snowshoeing combines fun with appreciation of the beauty of a winter landscape. The amount of exercise obtained from this increasingly popular winter sport can be adapted to the physical condition of the individual by modifying the distance covered or the type of terrain hiked. One hard 75-year-old snowshoer at Alta, Utah, climbs the lift line, straight uphill, daily all winter. This, however, would not be recommended for the average showshoer, especially at 9000 feet above sea level. Equally as much fun and exercise can be obtained when snowshoeing on level terrain.

The traditional snowshoe is made of thin strips of top-grade ash and rawhide in either a bearpaw or a Yukon (trail) style. The bearpaw design is an oval about 13" wide and 24" to 33" long. Although most bearpaw snowshoes are flat, some have turned up toes to reduce stubbing the tips or loading them with snow. This design is highly maneuverable in brush and woods but is not recommended for the beginner because of its width.

The Yukon, or trail, snowshoe is a teardrop or beavertail shape 10" to 14" wide and 44" to 56" long. The longer, narrower versions, although difficult to maneuver in heavily wooded areas, are extremely fast on open terrain. The beginner's version of this snowshoe is 10" wide and 48" long.

A good snowshoe contains three straps: a wide strap over the toe, a narrower, adjustable strap stretching from the toe strap around the heel and back to the toe, and a narrow strap over the instep. Although poles are not required for snowshoeing, the mature adult may find one or two ski poles or a single wooden pole useful for balance and security, especially if balance or mobility are problems.

Because ash and rawhide are increasingly difficult to obtain and expensive when used for snowshoes ($50 per set), plastic and nylon versions with neoprene straps are becoming increasingly popular ($15 per set). In addition to being practical and economical, these synthetic models are virtually indestructible.

Any normal winter apparel and footwear will suffice as clothing when snowshoeing. Several layers of clothing are recommended as this permits an easy adaptation of clothing to accommodate changing weather conditions. Warm mittens, hat, and goggles are necessary in extremely hostile conditions. Any high, warm, and well-fitted footwear will suffice. Commonly used are the standard, insulated, moccasin-toed work boots, snowmobile boots, army surplus boots, or hiking boots.

Anyone who can walk can snowshoe with ease if the following points are remembered:

1. Always set the tail, or heel, of the snowshoe down first.
2. As one snowshoe is set down, swing the other around and forward, keeping the toe up.
3. If the snowshoes are wide, a wider-than-normal stance will be needed to keep from stepping on the opposite snowshoe.

The blind or partially sighted snowshoer will find it easy to follow a snowshoer who has fastened bells to the snowshoe straps. The hearing impaired with no balance problems can learn to snowshoe with ease.

Snowshoeing should never be done alone, especially in wilderness areas. Most summer hiking trails are excellent for snowshoeing. It can even be fun for the beginner in a city park. Because breaking trail can be tiring, it is recommended that the lead snowshoer be alternated, especially in deep snow or on long hikes. In addition, only physically conditioned, experienced mature adults should go on long hikes in deep snow.

Remember to begin with short hikes on level terrain when this activity is first introduced into the program. The length of the hike should be increased slowly and in relation to the endurance of the group.

GOLF

Golf as an active sport can be enjoyed by most mature adults throughout life. In fact, most city, county, or state amateur golf associations sponsor annual championships for senior players. Such tournaments are usually arranged in classes, according to age (50-54, 55-59, 60-64, 65-69, 70 and older), and prizes are usually awarded for low gross and low net scores.

A variety of common modifications can permit the mature adult with low endurance or medical problems to enjoy some aspects of the game of golf. Electric golf carts can be used by players unable to walk nine holes, or the golfer can reduce the number of holes played. The reduction of holes played is best accomplished on courses where the fourth or fifth green is close to the clubhouse, making it easy for the player to leave the course. In addition, relatively flat courses should be selected for play. Further modifications might necessitate reducing the game to pitch-and-putt play around practice greens, to minature golf, or to driving-range practice.

As a group, mature adults who have participated in the game of golf for a reasonable period of time usually hit a straight and accurate ball. They may not, however, have the distance to their strokes that they experienced when they were younger players. If one observes 70- and 80-year-old golfers around greens, as a group they are exceptionally accurate with their short game.

Golf can be an enjoyable recreational pursuit for the arthritic if the hands can still grasp the club and the modifications mentioned above are utilized. Many city and county golf courses sell reduced-price memberships to older players who generally play during the daytime hours when other golfers are working.

TENNIS

Tennis is a suitable recreation activity for the mature adult who is an experienced player in good physical condition. In fact, there is an active 68-year-old tennis-tournament participant in Salt Lake City who is still playing doubles even after a serious heart attack, but with medical approval. After recovery from her heart attack, this player's medical doctor monitored her heart rate during an entire day of activity, which included tennis and bridge in addition to other daily household tasks. The most stressful readings on this monitor were recorded during a period behind the wheel of an automobile in congested traffic, indicating, at least for this individual, that the stresses of daily living can be greater than active participation in sports.

It should be emphasized that medical approval is essential for cardiac patients who participate in active sports. Paddle tennis (doubles) is an excellent substitute for the tennis enthusiast who must limit participation.

BOWLING

Most mature adults can enjoy bowling as a recreational pursuit with little or no modifications. For the bowler with limited arm strength, lighter-weight balls can be used. These balls should, however, be heavy enough to activate the automatic pin-setting machine.

Bowling is an excellent socialization sport. Tournaments are usually very stimulating for the group and can be set up in rounds of only one game, rather than the traditional three games, to permit participation by a greater number of bowlers who may lack the strength and stamina needed to roll three games.

Frequently, a group of mature adults can get reduced bowling rates during off hours. Balls and shoes can be rented at very nominal fees, and many bowling alleys, upon request, will also provide instruction for the group.

ROLLER SKATING

Roller skating can be an enjoyable, social recreation activity for many mature adults. As with ice skating, roller-skating rinks can usually be secured at reduced fees during off hours. These rinks do provide rental skates for use by the participants at very nominal fees.

Music is very useful in the development of roller-skating rhythm, especially if the skater is apprehensive. As with ice skating, holding hands is an excellent teaching technique for the beginner or partially sighted roller skater. This technique lends support to the apprehensive beginner, aids in the development of a proper rhythm, and provides security to the partially sighted. As with other sports, roller skating is not difficult for the mature adult with a hearing loss unless balance is a problem. The degree of hip or knee involvement of an arthritic will be the determining factor in roller-skating ability.

BOATING

Mature adults can enjoy a variety of boating activities. Large, stable, recreational-type craft present no problems to this population. Many of these craft even use ramps for boarding, permitting access for wheelchairs. These large craft provide a variety of services to the public, such as day or weekend cruises, which could be the highlights of the recreation program.

Use of small craft, such as canoes and rowboats, should be limited to individuals with swimming ability. Life jackets should be required and all standard safety procedures should be followed.

OTHER ACTIVITIES

Sports activities which usually require little, if any, modification for the mature adult include the following:

Activity	Possible Modification
Archery	Use lighter bow; reduce target distance
Badminton	Doubles recommended for those in poor physical condition

Activity	Possible Modification
Casting	Use chairs for those unable to stand for long periods of time; an excellent activity for those confined to wheelchairs
Croquet	Use larger wickets if necessary; paint wickets white so they can easily be seen
Dancing	Folk, square, social; modify by selecting moderate tempos, especially in folk and social dancing
Deck tennis	Doubles or team play recommended, except for those in good physical condition
Handball	Doubles recommended; only for experienced players in good physical condition
Horseshoes	Substitute rubber or plastic rings for use by individuals with extremely weak arms; excellent activity for those confined to wheelchairs
Racquetball	Doubles recommended; only for experienced players in good condition
Shuffleboard	Use longer-handled cues for individuals confined to wheelchairs; tournaments are stimulating
Softball	Recommended for those in moderately good condition
Squash rackets	Doubles recommended; only for experienced players in good physical condition
Table tennis	Can usually be played without modification; lowered table height permits participation by those in wheelchairs; tournaments are stimulating
Volleyball	Recommended for those in moderately good condition

EXERCISE

Most medical authorities agree that exercise is important, even for the older mature adult. Properly conducted experience programs will improve the efficiency of the various organs and systems of the body such as the digestive system and the cardiovascular system. When muscle tone is improved through exercise, posture and total body appearance can improve. In addition, when an exercise program is combined with a proper diet, overweight can be reduced and the maintenance of proper weight becomes easier. Because exercise promotes relaxation, it can also reduce the effects of mental fatigue, tension, strain, and boredom which are typically produced by twentieth-century living. Additional side effects include an individual who looks, feels, and functions more efficiently in daily living activities.

Exercise programs conducted by the average recreation program director should be low enough in intensity to be safe for the group of older mature adults included in the program. Care must be taken to avoid any potential cardiovascular strain. This is especially true when medical and physiological monitoring are not available. A physician should prescribe the appropriate regimen for each and every individual in the group. Even exercise programs of low to moderate intensity can be beneficial to the group in the sociopsychological domain. In addition, such programs will contribute to improved muscle tone and joint mobility and will help each individual participant regain and maintain flexibility, balance, coordination, and agility.

If exercises are properly selected, those individuals in wheelchairs, walkers, or with varying degrees of joint limitation due to arthritis can safely participate. Classes should be 30 to 40 minutes in length and contain a set of graduated exercises. The program should begin at a slow pace. Exercises should be made progressively more difficult, with the group setting the pace. If necessary, the group can be divided into skill levels so that exercises can be individualized. Musical accompaniment is excellent to set the pace for the group. The tempo, however, should be set to accommodate the slowest members of the group. When appropriate, members of the group can be used as leaders for some of the exercises.

Aerobic dance is becoming increasingly popular and is an excellent form of exercise that can be appropriately modified for a group of older mature adults. Swimming, discussed earlier in this chapter, is also an excellent fitness activity.

Exercise for Fitness

Although further study is needed, current research findings (deVries 1970 and 1976; Adams and deVries 1973; Wilson 1974; Coleman 1972; Barry et al. 1966; and Stamford 1972) tend to indicate that aerobic capacity can be improved from 10 to 30 percent in older people, even in those who have been sedentary most of their lives. This research also tends to indicate that major desirable physiological effects result from participation in quality exercise programs by the healthy mature adult and the cardiac patient. These benefits include increases in blood-vessel size, myocardial efficiency and work capacity, energy sources, arterial oxygen content, efficiency of peripheral blood distribution and return, tolerance to psyche-emotional stress; and decreases in heart rate, arterial blood pressure, vulnerability to shortness of breath, cholesterol levels, obesity and adiposity, and strain associated with psyche-emotional stress.

If exercise programs are to be of benefit to the cardiovascular system by increasing the oxygen-carrying capacity of the body's circulatory system, they must be of sufficient duration, frequency, and intensity to elevate the heart rate. Only when this is accomplished can aerobic capacity, or the individual's capacity to supply oxygen to the working muscles, be improved. The exercise program should, therefore, contain the following elements:

1. Medical supervision and assessment of the exercise tolerance level of each and every individual included in the program. Medical and physiological monitoring *must* be available if intense fitness programs are conducted for this segment of our population.
2. A quality program of physical activity for a minimum of 30 minutes, two or three times weekly.
   a. Begin with a short, initial warm-up of stretching flexibility exercises to prevent muscle and joint aches and pains and to gradually increase the heart rate.
   b. Finish with a short cool-down period to gradually decrease the heart rate.
3. Exercise of sufficient intensity to provide the participant with activity to at least 60 percent of his maximal exercise level and strenuous enough to produce a training effect. The participant's initial level of fitness determines his level of intensity.
4. The program should consist of several types of exercise.
   a. 25 to 30 minutes of calisthenics.
   b. 5 to 10 minutes of continuous and rhythmical activity such as walking/ jogging, cycling, or swimming. This activity, because it is specifically designed to elevate the heart rate to approximately 120 to 130 beats per minute, gradually increasing to 150 beats per minute as the individual's aerobic capacity increases, should be performed only when medical and physiological monitoring is available.
5. Music to set the pace and make the exercise sessions more enjoyable.

To determine how well sedentary men aged 49 to 65 would respond to endurance training, Dr. M. L. Pollock (1976) and other investigators at the Institute for Aerobics Research in Dallas, Texas, conducted a study involving a group of 22 trainees and a group of 8 controls. The training program met for 30 minutes, 3 days a week for 20 weeks and consisted of walking and jogging on a quarter-mile track, with the jogging distance increased progressively from the fourth to the twentieth week. Compared with the control group which showed no changes, those in the training group exhibited marked positive changes as follows: increased breathing efficiency and heart-action efficiency; and decreased heart rate at rest, blood pressure, body weight, skinfold fat, and abdominal girth. As a result of this study, the investigators reported that men over age 49 respond favorably to endurance exercise in the form of beneficial changes similar in magnitude to those found in previous studies with younger individuals.

Vigorous exercise programs, therefore, are both feasible and effective for bringing about cardiorespiratory fitness as measured by aerobic capacity or heart-rate/workload relationships even in normally healthy middle-aged and elderly men and women. If medical and physiological monitoring is not available, however, only mild to moderate exercise programs should be conducted only with medical approval. Such programs of physical activity should be designed to be safe, enjoyable, inexpensive, and nonseasonal and should fit easily into the individual's weekly schedule, allowing for a progressive increase in intensity of effort and permitting *all* participants to exercise success.

Fitness Program Guidelines

When conducting fitness programs for mature adults, medical approval for all participants is absolutely necessary. In addition, the activity supervisor *must:*

1. Have adequate knowledge of the structure and physiological functions of the human organism
2. Have adequate knowledge of motivational techniques
3. Understand emotional factors as related to stress
4. Be up-to-date on current fitness developments
5. Have adequate knowledge regarding the modification of the activities used to meet the specific needs of the individual so that activity modification and sequencing can be used to vary the demand requirements of the exercises
6. Carefully supervise the activity and be alert for any change in the condition of the participant that may indicate that the activity is too strenuous and immediate modifications are necessary
7. Have adequate knowledge to select and conduct exercises to meet each and every participant's exercise-intensity level as determined by the physician
8. Know immediate emergency care, including cardiopulmonary resuscitation techniques and related emergency procedures, and be up-to-date in training
9. *Not* permit any participant to go beyond his limits or capabilities as approved by his physician and his past exercise performance
10. Work closely with the physician, especially if excessively obese individuals are in the program
11. Avoid major heart-disease risk factors
12. Report signs of unusual stress or fatigue during exercise sessions to the physician
13. Establish and enforce safety procedures, especially regarding the use of equipment
14. Keep all exercise equipment in excellent condition
15. Modify or cancel the exercise program if the temperature and/or humidity are high in the exercise area, thus avoiding serious heat illness

Walking/Jogging

Jogging can be very strenuous on the back, feet, legs, hips, and knee joints of many mature adults. Unless the individual has participated in a jogging program throughout his or her life span, it is not recommended that the individual begin a fitness program by attempting to jog for any distance or time. Vigorous walking can be as effective for older individuals and is recommended as a starting point for the sedentary individual. When vigorous walking can be performed for 10 minutes without undesirable side effects, walking can be combined with jogging (example: walk 50 steps, jog 10 steps, repeat for 5 minutes). The walk/ jog can be made increasingly difficult by increasing the number of jog steps during the five-minute interval (example: walk 50 steps, jog 15 steps, repeat for 5 minutes). An excellent walk/jog progression is outlined in the Administration on Aging manual, *The Fitness Challenge in Later Years: An Exercise Program for Older Americans*, listed in the Selected References at the end of this chapter.

In all walking/jogging programs, if the participant experiences any trembling, nausea, extreme breathlessness, pounding in the head or pain in the chest, activity should be stopped immediately. These signs usually indicate that the individual's exercise tolerance level has been reached. Such information should be reported to the physician so that exercise modifications can be made and approved.

Cycling

Cycling is an excellent fitness-type activity for those mature adults who cannot safely participate in walking/jogging programs. The three-wheeler is a popular cycle with many seniors as it provides a greater degree of stability than the traditional two-wheeler. In fact, in Santa Ana, California, a 94-year-old great-grandmother participated in the American Cancer Society 1976 bike-a-thon using such a cycle.

As with other activities, when cycling is introduced into the recreation program the rides should be of short distance—one to two miles. The distance ridden should be gradually increased as the tolerance level of the individuals and the group improve.

The results of a cycling program conducted in Mesa, Arizona (Stone and Buccola, 1976), with 60- to 80-year-old retirees indicated that participation in a cycling program for a period of several months has the potential for producing the following benefits: increased physical fitness, increased flexibility, decreased body fat and body weight, and decreased blood pressure. An additional benefit included meeting the social needs of the participants by providing companionship and fun.

SENIOR OLYMPICS

Since its founding by Warren Blaney in 1969, the Senior Sports International has sponsored an annual International Senior Olympics. This series of athletic events is held in and around Los Angeles, California. The Senior Olympics was developed with the goals of promoting healthier, happier, and more productive lives for adults through sports. It recognizes the adult athlete by giving him or her the opportunity to experience the excitement of international championship competition.

Competition is offered in a wide variety of athletic events including: archery, badminton, basketball, billiards, bowling, boxing, curling, cycling, darts, fencing, frisbee, golf, gymnastics, handball, ice-skating (speed, hockey, dance), judo, karate, lacrosse, polo, powerlifting, racquetball, roller skating, rugby, soccer, softball, squash, surfing, swimming, table tennis, tennis, track and field, water polo, water skiing, and wrestling.

Although there is no top age limit for entrance in the Senior Olympics, to date the oldest competitor has been a youthful 79. Following are a few of the records for these events:

Harold Chapson	age 70	1500-meter run—time: 5:30.8
Hal Higdon	age 42	300-meter steeplechase—time: 9:30.0
Al Guidet	age 55	220-meter run—time: 0:23.6
Walt Westbrook	age 75	Two tennis titles in 100-degree heat
Ted Mumby	age 75	16 events in 3 different sports; won triple-jump event
Rod Drummond	age 66	Handball, racquetball, swimming, shotput, and discus events
Edith Mendyka	age 64	First in the javelin throw

A total of 2,500 athletes competed in the June 1975 Senior Olympics. Persons interested in additional information, including how to conduct a Senior Olympics program in their area, should contact Warren Blaney, Mutual of Omaha Building, 5225 Wilshire Boulevard, Suite 302, Los Angeles, California 90036.

SELECTED REFERENCES

Adams, G. M., and deVries, H. A. Physiological effects of an exercise training regimem upon women aged 52-79. *Journal of Gerontology*, 1973, *28*, 50-55.

Administration on Aging, U.S. Department of Health, Education and Welfare. *The fitness challenge in later years: An exercise program for older americans.* Publication no. OHD/AoA 73-20802. Washington, D.C.: U.S. Government Printing Office, 1973.

American Camping Association. Old age: A new frontier for camping. *Camping Magazine,* November, 1951.

Ansell, Charles. Camping for older adults. *Jewish Center Program Aids,* March 1953.

Barry, A. J.; Daly, J. W.; Pruett, E. D. R.; Steinmetz, J. R.; Page, H. F.; Birkhead, N. C.; and Rodahl, K. The effects of physical conditioning on older individuals. *Journal of Gerontology,* 1966, *21,* 182-191.

Berlin, Pearl. *The learning of swimming by senior citizens, a research project.* CNCA no. HTF/11-16-1966/IC, October 1960.

Brayer, Judith L. *Grandma and grandpa go to camp.* National Jewish Welfare Board, 145 East 32nd Street, New York, 1954.

Buccola, Victor A., and Stone, William J. Effects of jogging and cycling programs on physiological and personality variables in aged men. *Research Quarterly,* 1975, *46,* 134-139.

Carroll, Julian. Master swimming—A fitness program for older age groups. *Journal of the Canadian Association for Health, Physical Education, and Recreation,* 1972, *38* (6), 5-7.

Coleman, A. Eugene. Physical fitness for adults. *American Corrective Therapy Journal,* May-June 1972, 63-67.

Deininger, LeRoy. Senior citizens go to camp. *International Journal of Religious Education,* March 1963.

Detroit Recreation Camp. *Senior citizen camp staff manual.* City of Detroit, Detroit Recreation Camp, 735 Randolf Street, Detroit, Michigan, 1961.

deVries, Herbert A. Fitness after fifty. *Journal of Health, Physical Education, and Recreation,* 1976, April, 47-49.

deVries, Herbert A. Physiological effects of an exercise training regimen upon men aged 52-88. *Journal of Gerontology,* 1970, *25,* 325-336.

Farmer, E. D. Foundation of Texas. Golden age camps prove huge success. *Your Age,* Author, Fort Worth, Texas (no date).

Frekany, George A., and Leslie, David A. Developing an exercise program for senior citizens. *Therapeutic Recreation Journal,* 1974, *8,* (4), 178-180.

Glascock, Martha McClain, and Scholer, E. A. Camping for older adults. *Camping Magazine,* 1969, *41,* 15-16.

Guerard, Ed. Steps in organizing a senior citizen camp. *Camping Magazine,* 1973, *45,* 26, 30.

Hanley, James R. It's olympic time for old athletes. *Salt Lake Tribune,* Magazine Section, p. 17, March 9, 1975.

Herbert, William G., and Herbert, David L. Exercise testing in adults: Legal and procedural considerations for the physical educator and exercise specialist. *Journal of Health, Physical Education, and Recreation,* 1975, *6,* 17-19.

Hochheimer, Rita. How senior citizens enrich the camp program. *Camping Magazine*, 1963, *35*, 17.

King, Frances, and Herzig, William E. *Golden age exercises.* New York: Crown, 1968.

Lemire, Clemet M. Senior citizens bowling. *Parks and Recreation*, 1967, *2*, (5), 33, 64-65.

Margolin, Lillian. What your camp can do for older adults. *Camping Magazine*, 1972, *44*, 10.

McLure, John W., and Leslie, David K. Guidelines for an exercise program leader for senior citizens. *Journal of Health, Physical Education, and Recreation*, 1972, *11*, 73-75.

Moore, Samuel A.; Smith, Julian W.; and Schuette, Fred J. Outdoor activities for older folk. *Journal of Health, Physical Education, and Recreation*, 1975, *11*, 59.

Moran, Joan M., and Kalakian, Leonard H. *Movement experiences for the mentally retarded or emotionally disturbed child.* Minneapolis: Burgess, 1977.

National Recreation and Park Association. Camping for seniors. *Recreation*, 1962, *55*, 236-237.

Pollock, M. L. Fitness training for men over 49. *Journal of the American Geriatrics Society*, 1976, *24*, 97.

Rand, Abby. Alf Engen: Portrait of a professional athlete at 64. *American Airlines Magazine*, December 1974, 20-23.

Sitarz, Dan. Tracks of the bigfoot—How to leave 'em. *Colorado High Country*, December 17, 1975, 6-7.

Skole, Robert. Cross country competition Scandinavian style: The older boys vs. the younger old boys. *The Physician and Sportsmedicine*, 1976, *4*, (2) 97, 99.

Stamford, B. A. Physiological effects of training upon institutionalized geriatric men. *Journal of Gerontology*, 1972, *27*, 451-455.

Stone, William J., and Buccola, Victor A. A cycling program for senior citizens. *Journal of Health, Physical Education, and Recreation*, April 1976, 63.

Van Der Smissen, Betty. Legal aspects of adult fitness programs. *Journal of Health, Physical Education, and Recreation*, February 1974, 54-56.

Wilson, Philip K. Cardiac rehabilitation program. *Journal of Health, Physical Education, and Recreation*, February 1974, 47-48, 53-54.

Wilson, Philip K., ed. *Adult fitness and cardiac rehabilitation.* Baltimore: University Park Press, 1975.

7
CREATIVE ARTS
AND CRAFTS

My heart leaps up when I behold
a rainbow in the sky:
So was it when my life began,
So is it now I am a man,
So be it when I shall grow old.
—William Wordsworth

Creativity is a human condition that inspires the feelings necessary to produce, form, or bring to pass a work of thought or imagination which is new or different. Because creativity is based on an individual's total past experiences with people, things, and events, many mature adults have a wealth of untapped creative powers. The recreation director should, therefore, include a variety of aesthetic and cultural activities in the organized recreation program for this group.

Frequently, encouragement and stimulation are necessary before the creativity of the individual or the group emerges. Planned trips to art museums and theatrical and musical productions can provide stimulation and bring enrichment into the lives of many mature adults. Discussion groups evolving from these experiences may aid in bringing the talents of members of the group to the surface. Deeper involvement with the arts can evolve if opportunity is provided for interested members to serve as volunteers for the arts, or members of the recreation program can plan and produce their own little theatre-type productions in music or drama. Among the regular participants in an organized recreation program, there may be experienced, retired professionals who are qualified to organize and direct such music or drama functions. Final productions should be open to the public for added group stimulation and motivation.

Because art is skill in performance that is acquired by experience, study, or observation, anything done well is an art. Therefore, opportunity should be provided to participate in as wide a variety of activities as space and facilities can accommodate. Painting, drawing, photography, sculpture, music, dance, drama, intellectual endeavors, and crafts of all types are but a few of the many possible art forms with program potential.

Frequently, members of the recreation group have the talent necessary to provide instruction in these various art forms to other interested mature adults. If necessary, however, outside instructional staff can be brought in for introductory lessons. Many professionals may willingly provide this service on a volunteer basis or at a very nominal fee. Or interested persons should be bused to organized classes offered in the community. The stimulation and enthusiasm that may result from such efforts is more than worth any expense that may be involved.

Because creativity is developed, not taught, several structured craft activities, with potential for creativity, are included in this chapter. All of the following craft activities are practical, usable, or sellable. Numerous other structured crafts, such as weaving, stitchery, copper tooling, and leather craft, could be included in the recreation program. All art and craft items produced by a group of mature adults could be sold at a recreation-center craft store, a church bazaar, or a booth at a local fair. The proceeds can be used to purchase additional craft supplies for the individual or the group.

MOSAICS

A mosaic is any decoration made by fitting together small pieces of colored gravel, colored glass, stone, tile, or other materials. These materials are usually cemented to some surface, such as wood or metal, the spaces between are filled with grout, and a grout sealer is applied to the grout surface.

Mosaic tiles are available in most art and craft stores in a variety of textures, shapes, sizes, and colors. They can be cut or arranged to fit any space and laid in curved or straight lines to form any shape. Work with mosaics is a rewarding hobby that is pleasant and relaxing, and it results in decorative and useful objects of beauty and art. Mosaic work can be made as simple or complex as the talents and abilities of the craftsperson, and it provides the mature adult with an opportunity to design and create beautiful items to use at home, to give as gifts, or to sell for profit. Typical mosaic items include table tops, wall murals, plaques, pictures, trivets, ash trays, and bowls.

Preparing Surface

If a metal surface is used for the mosaic design, it should be rustproof, clean, and dry. If an old table is used as the mosaic surface, it should be cleaned thoroughly to remove all wax and grease. Pasta-Solve is excellent for this purpose; it should be applied and allowed to soak for one to two hours before wiping clean. The surface of cleaned or new wood should then be sealed with a thin brush coat of varnish to prevent any warping that may occur from water in the grout. Allow to dry thoroughly before applying tiles.

Working Design

The pattern or design to be created should be worked out in advance, preferably on a piece of heavy wrapping paper that has been cut to the exact size of the surface. When the final design has been determined, carbon paper should be placed on the surface, carbon side down; the paper design should then be taped flat on top of the surface. Trace the pattern onto the surface, then remove the paper and carbon. Place masking tape around edges to protect wood or metal from glue and wet grout. Next, begin gluing tile directly in place on the surface. All-purpose white glue or contact cement are excellent for gluing the tile.

Gluing

When placing tile, fill in straight lines and outlines of designs first. When laying tile straight, lay one row at a time, keeping rows even and spacing between tiles uniform. When laying tiles along a curve or circle, keep rows even. Leave wedge-shaped spaces between tiles, with inner corners nearly touching. Complete the main portion of the design next, working from the outline toward the center. Next, fill in the background, working from the outer edge toward the design. Cut tiles to fit when necessary. When filling designs or background, lay tiles carefully, conforming them to the overall style and pattern of the design.

Grouting

Tiles should be placed on the surface as evenly spaced as possible and approximately $\frac{1}{16}$ of an inch apart. This space is filled with grouting after the glue has dried thoroughly. Before grouting, cover any exposed wood edging with masking tape. Mix grout with water to a consistency of thick cake frosting. Spoon or pour grout onto the tile, then rub into the spaces between the tiles. If grout becomes dry while working on the project, mositen hands or brush the surface with water to soften the grout and permit the hands to continually work the grout into spaces between the tiles. Rub for approximately 15 minutes, or until all air bubbles are worked out. Let the grout set for 30 minutes and then wipe off the excess with a damp cloth; dry slowly for approximately 45 minutes.

Finishing

Polish with a soft, dry cloth or paper towel to remove any excess grout. Apply grout sealer to protect the finished surface. Rub the surface of the tile to bring up natural sheen. Tile and grout cleaner can be used for this purpose. If necessary, use 000 steel wool to remove any grout from exposed wood or metal.

MACRAMÉ

Macramé, or the art of knot tying, is more than 2000 years old. It is a current decorating fad used to make plant hangers, belts, wall hangings, screens, and shades.

Any type of cord, from heavy upholstery cord to light-weight string or thread can be used for macramé. For best results, however, a tightly woven or braided cord strong enough to withstand tying and pulling and firm enough to provide tension for shapely knots should be used. Examples of such cord are nylon seine, mason's cord, parachute cord, Holland sisal, cotton twine, and seine cord. Heavy-weight sisal is excellent for practicing knots because it permits the beginner to make an even knot with little difficulty and enables the beginner to produce a finished product quickly. Mistakes are easy to detect and easy to untie.

Only a few supplies are needed to make a simple macramé project such as a plant hanger: scissors, cord, masking tape to bind cord ends to prevent fraying, and white glue to fasten cut ends and splice short cords. For fancy plant hangers, wood beads and wood rings are frequently added.

The following steps should be used to estimate the cord length needed for a project:
1. Measure and mark a length of cord 30" long.
2. Tie a knotting sample 2" to 4" long.
3. Measure the cord remaining to determine length used for knotting. For example: if 24" of cord was used to make 4" of knots, each inch of knotting 'requires 6" of cord.

Because loops on knots and spaces between knots can use large amounts of cord, a generous amount of additional cord should be added to the estimated length when cutting the cord.

When an error is made in estimating cord length or when a longer project is desired, more cord can be added by using the following techniques.

If you are working with twisted cord:
1. Untwist the cord ends that are to be joined and cut them at staggered lengths.
2. Lay new cord on the ends of cord being worked. Twist the ends together so one even length is achieved.
3. Glue the joined sections to hold.
4. Allow to dry before working cord.

When tying knots, pull them tight as they are worked and keep them as uniform as possible. This is especially important when tying symmetrical knots such as square knots and Josephine knots.

When mastered, the following knots can be used alone, or in various combinations, to make a variety of decorative and useful macrame projects.

Starting Knots

The lark's head knot is usually worked in a series around a cord, dowel, or similarly stable unit called a holding line. Use to start work when keeping an exact width is not important.

A. Place knot loosely on holding   B. Pull knot tight.
    line.

Lark's head knot

The double-clove hitch with picot is usually worked in a series around a holding line.

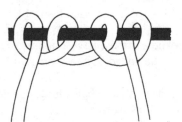

A. Slip a lark's head backward   B. Pull knot tight with center
    around holding line; loop   loop at top forming picot.
    cord ends around holding
    line to form half hitches.

Double-clove hitch with picot

Basic Knots and Variations

The half hitch is a simple turn used in chains and braids. A half hitch can be worked in either direction.

Half hitch

An alternating half-hitch braid is worked with four strands. Using strand 1 as a tying cord, tie a half hitch around strands 2 and 3. Next, use strand 4 to tie a half hitch around strands 3 and 2. Repeat, alternating strands 1 and 4.

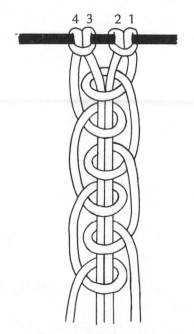

Alternating half-hitch braid

The clove hitch knot is actually two half hitches. Clove hitches are used to strengthen work and stiffed edges.

Clove hitch

The alternating clove-hitch braid is worked with four strands. Use strand 1 to tie a clove hitch around anchor cords 2 and 3. Next, use strand 4 to tie a clove hitch around strands 3 and 2. Repeat, alternating strands 1 and 4.

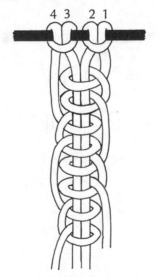

Alternating clove-hitch braid

The half square knot is worked with four strands. Place strand 1 under strands 2 and 3; bring strand 4 under strand 1, over strands 3 and 2, and through loop as shown in the diagram. Pull cords tight.

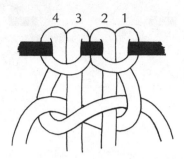

Half square knot

The spiral half-square-knot braid is worked by tying a series of six half square knots. Be sure to keep strands 1 and 4 going in the same direction. This braid will automatically spiral around its anchor strands as it is worked.

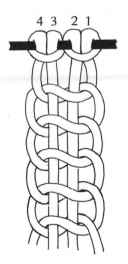

Spiral half-square-knot braid

The square knot is worked with four strands of cord.

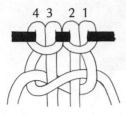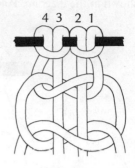

A.   Place strand 1 under strands
2 and 3; hold; bring strand
4 under 1, over 3 and 2, through
loop at right; pull tight.

B.   Place strand 4 over 2 and 3;
hold; bring strand 1 over 4,
under 3 and 2, through loop
at right.

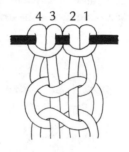

C.   Pull tight.

Square knot

The square-knot braid is a series of square knots.

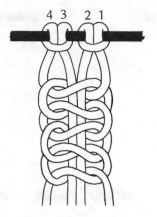

Square-knot braid

The looped square-knot braid is a series of square knots with loops formed on the outer edges by working the cord around a dowel or pencil.

Looped square-knot braid

The Josephine knot is worked with two strands of cord looped over a holding line.

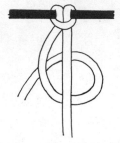

A. Make a loop with strand 1 and lay strand 2 over it.

B. Bring strand 2 under leg of loop and over strand 1.

C. Continue weaving strand 2 through, completing first knot.

D. Loop strand 1 again to right, but the reverse of loop in step A, with strand 2 under loop.

E. Complete second knot; repeat pairs of knots in same sequence.

Josephine knot

The overhand knot is usually used at cord ends to prevent fraying.

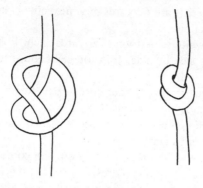

Overhand knot

The gathering cord is used to start work when a holding line is not used. It is also used to join cords when work is finished.

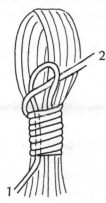

A. Fold one end of gathering cord into a loop; hold end and loop base secure and wrap cord around loop; place end 2 inside loop.

B. Pull end 1 until loop and end 2 are inside gathering cord; clip off ends.

Gathering cord

Directions for Plant Hanger Using Knots Included in This Chapter

The plant-hanger project is worked from the top and is approximately 48"
long. The necessary materials are 62 yards of white seine twine. Proceed according to the following directions:

1. Cut eight cords of white seine twine 7½ yards each. Fold all cords in half,
   placing loops neatly side by side. Join the eight loops together with a 24"
   length of gathering cord.
2. Arrange cords in four groups of four cords each. Repeat following instructions for each group of four cords. Note: It is easier to work one set of
   cords at a time, rolling the other sets into a ball and securing with a plastic
   bag twister until ready to work.
3. Of the four cords being worked, the two outside cords are knotting cords
   and the two inside cords are filler cords.
4. Approximately 2" down from gathering cord spiral, tie a square knot. Tie
   four more square knots, spacing each knot 1" apart (five knots).
5. Skip down 2" and tie twelve half knots (spiral half square knot braid).
6. Skip down 2" and tie five consecutive square knots (square knot braid).
7. Skip down 2" and tie twelve half knots (spiral half square knot braid).
8. Skip down 2" and tie five consecutive square knots with loops at the outer
   edges (looped square knot braid).
9. Skip down 2" and tie twelve half knots (spiral half knot braid).
10. Repeat steps 4 through 9 on the other three groups of cords. Keep space
    and knots on all sets of cord even.
11. Skip down 6". Use the right two cords of one group of cords and the left
    two cords of the next group of cords to make a square knot. Repeat three
    more times until all cords are joined.
12. Skip down 6". Secure all cords together, using the gathering technique or
    one large overhand knot made with all sixteen cords.
13. Cut all cords to measure 8" in length from knot executed in step 12. Cords
    can be unraveled to form a tassel, or even cord end can be secured with an
    overhand knot.

BASKETRY

The same techniques are used today in basketry weaving that people used
centuries ago to weave household items. Baskets are especially popular today
with macrame plant hangers.

The supplies needed for basketry are frames and reed or raffia. These supplies can be purchased at most art supply shops. The frame selected will determine the general shape of the basket to be produced.

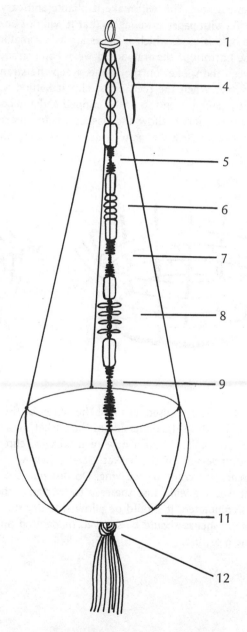

Sample plant hanger

Before weaving, the reed or raffia should be soaked for approximately 30 minutes in warm water. This will make it pliable and easy to handle. Next, dry the reed or raffia with paper toweling so that it will not be soaking wet.

If a large base is used, which is necessary when making a tall basket, begin weaving at the bottom of the frame and weave one strand of reed at a time, in and out between the spokes on the frame. Keep the strands of reed as close together as possible. When the reed ends, clip it behind a spoke and begin with another reed by laying it on top of the clipped end and continue weaving. When the weaving is completed, allow the basket to dry thoroughly, then spray or paint it with a coat of clear shellac to seal out dirt, heat, and moisture.

If a flat, low frame is used, begin at the center of the frame, plait the end of the reed behind and on the underside of the basket, weaving the reed in and out between the spokes. To begin a new reed weaver, clip the old reed behind a spoke on the underside of the basket. Start a new weaver by placing it beside the clipped end and continue weaving. Do not pull the reed too tightly as extremely tight weaving will cause the reed to overlap as the rows are made. When the basket is completed, it should be allowed to dry thoroughly. Then a coat of clear lacquer or shellac should be sprayed or painted on both sides to seal out dirt, heat, and moisture.

WOOD CRAFTS

Wood crafts are enjoyed by most men and many women who participate in recreation-center programs. The projects included on the following pages are quite appropriate with the current house-plant craze. They can all be made with minimum tools—saw, drill, screws, screwdriver, dowels, wood, and varnish or paint. All of these projects are practical as household items, gifts, or bazaar items.

For safe and efficient operation, all tools should be kept in proper repair and should be sharp, clean, and adequately lubricated. If power tools are used, proper apparel should be worn (no loose clothing or jewelry), including safety glasses and dust masks when appropriate. The work area should be clean and free of all hazards. Most power tools come with a list of safe operating procedures which should be strictly observed. In addition, always conform to the following guidelines:

1. The proper tool should be used for the designated task.
2. Materials being worked on should be properly secured with clamps or a vise, not with the hands or feet.
3. The hands and other parts of the body should be kept away from the working parts of the tool.
4. Only persons with good eyesight and steady hands should be permitted to use power tools.
5. Before power tools are used, they should be checked to insure that all adjustable parts are properly tightened.
6. All power tools should be properly insulated, and extension cords must be of adequate size to prevent loss of power and overheating.

Plywood Trivet

To make a plywood trivet, cut ½" plywood into ¾"-wide strips. From the strips, cut a ½" length; lay down with edge-grain up. Around it glue three 1" lengths and one 1½" length, using white glue. Continue to add pieces of increasing lengths to form a 7" square design, or larger if desired. Sand all surfaces smooth. Soak in vegetable oil.

Children's Building Blocks and Puzzle

To make the children's building blocks, cut eleven 3" by 3" square block from a 2 by 4. Cut square blocks as illustrated in the diagram—the dark circles are holes for dowels. Or creatively cut the blocks into puzzle pieces. Cut a 1" dowel into three pieces, each 3" long.

A tray for the blocks can be made by using a 9" by 12" by 1" shelving board and adding 1" by 2" strips as sides. Attach the sides to the bottom with glue and finishing nails.

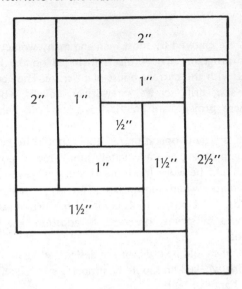

Plywood trivet

To finish the blocks and tray, sand all edges smooth. Varnish or paint with nontoxic enamel paint, or leave unfinished. Arrange the blocks in the tray. They can be used as a puzzle or as a set of building blocks.

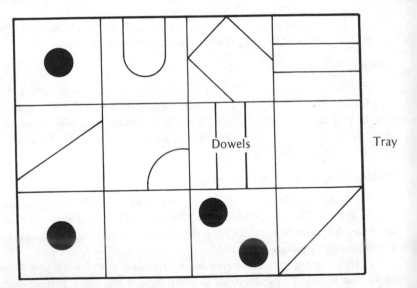

Children's building blocks and tray

Holders from Dowels

A variety of useful small holders can be made from pieces of 1½" dowels.

Pen holder. To make a pen holder, drill holes for pens and pencils in one end of a 3" length of dowel; then sand, wax, or varnish; finally, glue felt on the opposite end for the bottom. Place pencils in the holes.

Pen holder

Letter holder. A letter holder can be made from a 6" length of dowel by planing one side flat and sawing slits in the other side; then sand, wax, or varnish. Glue felt on the flat side and place letters in the slits.

Letter holder

Candleholder. Make a candleholder by planing one side and drilling holes in the opposite side of a 6" length of dowel. Finish by sanding, waxing, or varnishing. Glue felt on the flat side and place candles in the holes.

Candleholder

Wall-Peg Plant Hanger

Use a 2" by 3" by 24" board for the back of the wall-peg plant hanger. Cut a ¾" dowel into three pieces, each 9" long, for the plant hangers. Cut a notch in the dowels to hold the planters (see diagram).

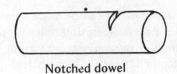

Notched dowel

Assemble the plant hanger by drilling holes for the dowels and mounting as illustrated in the diagram.

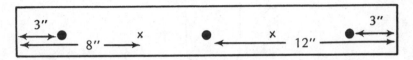

Pound the dowels securely into the holes. Round off all corners; then sand, stain, and varnish.

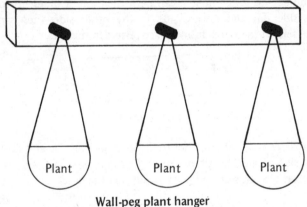

Wall-peg plant hanger

Orange-Crate-Type Plant Shelf

An attractive and useful orange-crate-type plant shelf can be made simply and inexpensively. Use a 1" by 8" by 24" board for the back. For the two sides use six strips of side lattice, each 24" long by 1⅜" wide. Use three strips for each side. The top, middle, and bottom shelves will require three pieces of wood, each 1" by 8" by 8".

To assemble, first sand all pieces; then drill two holes in back, approximately 3" from the sides and top, for hanging nails. Glue and nail as illustrated. Finish with a stain and varnish.

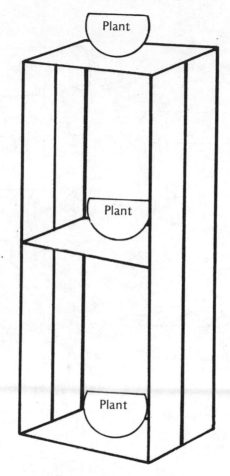

Orange-crate-type plant shelf

Dowel Toys

Using a little creative imagination and dowels ranging in size from $\frac{1}{8}$" to $1\frac{1}{2}$", a variety of animals and toys can be made. After assembling the animals, they can be sanded and stained or painted with a nontoxic enamel paint. Yarn and felt can be added for tails and ears.

Giraffe

Elephant

Rhino

Camel

Hippo

Gator

Train—connect cars
with screw hooks

Dowel toys

Ice-Cream-Stick (Slapstick) Trivet

The ice-cream-stick trivet is a useful item and makes a practical gift. The necessary materials are 33 ice-cream sticks, 33 small wood beads, and 1 yard of thread-type elastic.

To assemble the trivet, drill two small holes in each stick: one hole in the middle of the stick and one hole ¼" from the end. If desired, paint or stain the sticks. Thread elastic through all of the end holes in the sticks; pull the elastic snug and tie. Thread the elastic alternately through the middle holes of the sticks and the wood beads. Pull the elastic snug but not tight—don't let the trivet buckle—and tie.

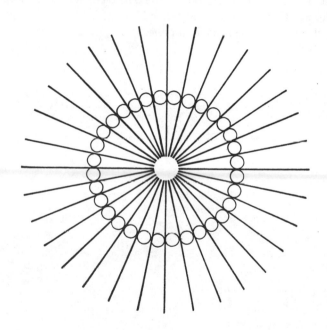

Ice-cream-stick (slapstick) trivet

COOLIE HAT

Since many mature adults dislike the sun, a coolie hat is a simple, useful craft that can be made when the group needs a break from other activities. Materials needed include a heavy, colorful wallpaper; cord, yarn, or ribbon; paste or a stapler; scissors; and shellac. Proceed with the following step-by-step directions.

1. Draw a circle with a 10" radius on the wallpaper.
2. Cut out the circle.
3. Make a 10" slit from the outside edge of the circle to its center (diagram 1).
4. Overlap the slit edge a few inches and paste or staple in place (diagram 2).
5. Cut or punch a hole 6" from the edge of the hat, on both sides (diagram 1).
6. Reinforce the holes with heavy tape.
7. Insert cord, yarn, or ribbon of sufficient length to tie under chin into each hole; tie a large knot in each cord on the outside of the hat to keep the cord from slipping through the hole (diagram 3).
8. Shellac the entire hat to make it durable.

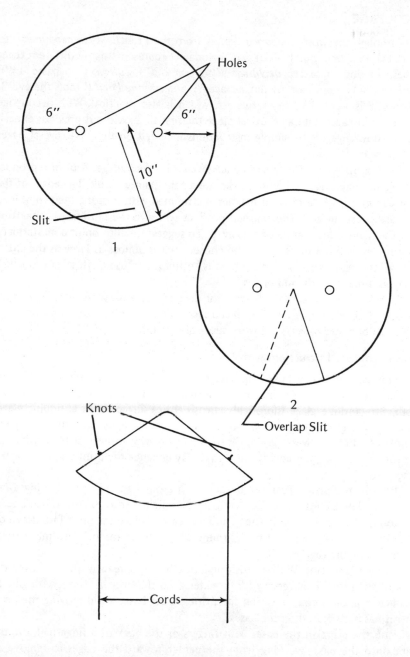

Holes

6"

6"

10"

Slit

1

2

Overlap Slit

Knots

Cords

Coolie hat

DECOUPAGE

Although the word *decoupage* stems from the French words *decouper* ("to cut out") and *decouput* ("a cut out"), today it represents many different techniques. Among these are *dechirage* ("to tear out"), *collage* ("to paste up"), *montage* ("a combination of flat surfaces"), and *trompe l'oeil* ("fools the eye"). Decoupage is a creative, decorative art, which is also practical. With decoupage an individual can create a beautiful piece the first time, without previous experince or knowledge, if the simple instructions included on the next several pages are followed.

Several different effects can be achieved with decoupage. A print reproduction from a painting can be used to create a hand-painted look. The edges of the print can be torn in a random manner or trimmed with scissors, then combined with a distress surface. The finished product will give the illusion of a painting with the rich mellow patina of antiquity. To suggest the illusion of a masterpiece painting on wood, a print should be chosen that is almost as large as the entire area of the article to be covered. This technique is used effectively on wall hangings, bread boards, and boxes.

The following materials needed for decoupage: a wooden surface, a print, antique glaze, decoupage finish, decoupage thinner, white glue, sand paper, a soft cloth or paper towel, steel wool, and paint brushes.

Basic Decoupage Instructions with Torn Prints

Prepare wooden surface. The base to which the print will be glued must be smooth. If necessary, sandpaper the surface and remove all dust with a soft cloth. Stir antique glaze thoroughly. Brush entire surface with antiquing glaze, following the grain of the wood. To remove excess glaze, use a cloth and wipe in the direction of the wood grain. Clean the brush with thinner or turpentine. Or the surface can be painted any color that may enhance the print selected for the decoupage.

Prepare the print. Tear the border from around the print by tearing away from you. For an antique effect, actually tear slightly into the print. Make tears of varying sizes and shapes. When finished tearing, place the print face down on an old surface. Sandpaper in back around the edges of the print to make them thinner and more ragged.

Adhere the print. With a brush or index finger, spread white glue over the back of the print. If necessary, drop water onto the print and mix with glue to produce a smooth coat. Position the print on the base, avoid moving the print after it has been placed on the base.

Rub the print on the base. With fingers or the back of a fingernail, rub the print onto the base, working from the center toward the edges to remove all wrinkles and air bubbles. A small brayer or roller is excellent for smoothing out

the print. When cutouts are used, wax paper should be placed between the print and the roller. If an air bubble cannot be removed by rubbing, prick the bubble with a pin, allow the air to escape, then rub again. Blot out excess glue from around the print with a damp cloth. The glue will dry clear, but large bumpy areas or spots need to be removed. This is especially important when working with cutouts. Clean the brush with water.

Seal the print. Because some inks are not compatible with decoupage finishes, always test a scrap piece or small corner of the print. Apply finish to the surface of the test piece. If the finish removes, blurs, or streaks the picture, seal the print by brushing a coat of white glue, thinned 25 percent with water, over the surface of the print. Brush it out thoroughly. (An unusual mottled or stippled background may be created by sealing entire article with glue thinned 50 percent with water. Brush the sealer on once—do not brush over surface repeatedly. The glue will bead as it dries.) Allow to dry until completely clear. Clean brush with water. Following the grain of the wood, brush a coat of finish onto the article with long, flowing strokes. If you do not wish to distress or antique the surface, the project is complete. Clean the brush with thinner.

Distress the surface. Distressing the surface of a wooden article makes it look as if it were a product of the ravages of time, use, and weather. If an antique effect is preferred, distress surface slightly and liberally. All or a few of the following suggestions may be used to make an article appear to be an antique. Strike the article with the edge of a blunt end of a hammer. Beat it with a chain. Dig into, scratch, or strike the surface with a screwdriver. Sandpaper areas of the surface lightly to remove sections of the print. Marks left by nails or small screws may be used to simulate worm holes. Finally, gouge out or chisel away areas of wood, especially around the outside edges of the article, with a wood gouge or paring knife.

Antique the surface. If an antique surface is desired, stir the antiquing glaze thoroughly and apply to the article with a brush or cloth, following the grain of the wood. Let the glaze dry approximately five minutes, then wipe with a soft cloth, using many small strokes in the direction of the grain of the wood to obtain an antique effect. A better antique effect will be achieved if more glaze is wiped off of the print than off of the edges and sides of the surface. If the antiquing glaze does not wipe off as desired, dampen a cloth with turpentine and gently wipe dark areas. Clean the brush with thinner or turpentine.

Finish the surface. If the surface of the article has been distressed or antiqued, an additional coat of finish will need to be applied. Brush finish on the article, following the grain of wood. Clean the brush with thinner. Allow the project to dry. Rub the surface with steel wool until all gloss has disappeared. Buff with a soft cloth. If the article is a wall plaque, it can be hung immediately. If it is a box or similar article, it should be allowed to dry for approximately two weeks before being used.

Other Decoupage Techniques

By slightly altering the basic instructions included above, a variety of interesting projects can be created.

Cutouts. It is simple to cut out and completely sink a print so that the edges of the print cannot be felt and only the design is apparent. This technique permits the creator to redesign the print.

1. If necessary, seal the print before cutting. (See Seal the Print section in basic instructions.)
2. Reinforce weak areas in the print, such as narrow stems on flowers, by drawing a line with a vivid-colored pencil to bridge the weak and strong points. When cutting out the print, these bridged areas should be cut last.
3. Define the contours of the figures in the print as the print is cut, so that hair is bushy like hair, wood is rough, and stone is smooth.
4. Smooth glue on decoupage surface (not on print), adding drops of water when necessary to ensure a smooth surface. Press each piece of the print as flat as possible with the fingers. (See basic instructions from Rub the Print on the Base section and continue through the end of the basic procedure.)
5. When decoupaging a box, glue one side at a time and try to integrate the design (i.e., flower stems trail around box), but do not glue one layer on top of another.
6. Build up the finish on the surface in at least six layers, dry, and then sand smooth. Repeat if necessary so that the surface and the print are level. Sanding should be done lightly to prevent damage to the design. Follow basic instructions to complete.

Engravings. Engravings can be added to a design by using colored pencils that blend with the colors in the print. This technique is frequently used to make a border or frame around the design.

Gold Filigree. Gold braid or gold medallions can be added to a design for highlights as a border or frame.

Trompe l'Oeil. A *trompe l'oeil* effect can be achieved by adding shadows to a creation to give it depth and to tie together different objects in the design.

Miscellaneous. For a delicate design, use very thin paper—such as origami paper—for a cutout. Marbleized or fresco papers can also be used to produce fascinating effects.

Collage. A collage with an interesting three-dimensional surface can be achieved by making an artistic composition of diverse materials such as dried flowers or ferns, embossed paper, pieces of wood, and nails.

Surface. The basic decoupage techniques can be applied to a variety of surfaces including metal, cork, glass, mirror, and plastic.

8
STAFF—PROFESSIONAL AND VOLUNTEER

There is a destiny that makes us brothers,
None goes his way alone.
All that we send into the lives of others,
Comes back into our own.
—Edwin Markham

In most communities across the nation, social and recreational activity groups exist exclusively and specifically for the older segment of our population. Such activity groups, called by a variety of names, meet under various auspices and sponsorships and have programs ranging in complexity from simple to diverse. The groups use a variety of existing or specially built facilities and are conducted by professional, volunteer, or group leadership.

Although qualified professional staff and volunteers are an important aspect of successful programming in such facilities, these professionals should assume few direct leadership roles and function primarily as program facilitators and resource consultants. Activity programs for mature adults cannot succeed unless the older participants, themselves, are actively involved in both the planning and leadership of the various scheduled and spontaneous activities that occur. Skillful leadership will facilitate this type of complete participant involvement in all aspects of the social and recreational program, thus insuring that the total sociological, psychological and physiological needs of each and every participant are adequately met.

Professional and volunteer staff do not need new bodies of knowledge to work successfully in such programs. What is needed, however, is skill in applying

138

existing basic knowledge and techniques to the distinct needs, interests, and desires of our population.

QUALIFICATIONS FOR PROFESSIONAL RECREATION STAFF

The basic qualification for the professional recreation staff is a degree in therapeutic recreation from an accredited institution of higher education, including field work and internship experience with mature adults. In addition, the successful professional recreator working in social and recreation activity programs for mature adults possesses a sincere interest in and desire to work with the older segment of our population. This ultimately implies an in-depth knowledge and understanding of the sociological, physiological, and psychological characteristics of this diverse segment of our population, including the healthy and active aged and the ill or disabled aged. An additional prerequisite would be an understanding of and ability to cope with the diverse attitudes toward life in general and leisure in particular that may be exhibited by members of this heterogeneous group of mature adults. This quality should be combined with a deep sensitivity to the needs, feelings, and desires of the individual participant and the group. Such a sincere professional would have a friendly, outgoing personality combined with the ability to bring warmth and enthusiasm to his or her work.

As a person, the professional recreator should recognize meaningful activity as a necessary element that should be included in the total life-style of all members of the society and have strong convictions regarding the values of leisure activity for mature adults. The professional recreator must regard recreation as an extremely important aid to growing old gracefully and believe that people who stay young despite their years do so because of active interests that provide satisfaction through participation.

A genuine enthusiasm and conscientiousness in all aspects of the work, including the professional growth of self and the leisure growth of the clients, is essential. These qualities should be combined with a sincere and honest sense of humor, including the ability to laugh with and not at the successes and failures of all mature adults participating in scheduled and spontaneous activity programs.

The professional recreator must possess skills in a wide variety of activities and be able to teach these skills to all mature adults who are a part of the total social and recreation activity program. When working on an individual or group basis in the development or refinement of skills and talents, patience is essential. This is especially true when it becomes necessary to teach and reteach an activity or separate the components of a skill into smaller, easier-to-learn parts. Imagination and initiative are the key elements to success in many teaching/learning situations, particularly when activities must be modified or adapted to facilitate handicapped individuals. Specific criteria for the selection of activities are included in chapter 9, Programming for Community Recreation Centers, Social Clubs, Retirement Communities; and chapter 10, Programming for Extended-Care Facilities.

In most cases the recreator will discover that the achievement of success in one activity by the mature adult can generate interest and participation in other activities, especially when this success is combined with an increased interest in self and others.

The ability to motivate or channel the interests of the individual or group is extremely important. Motivation may be needed to stimulate within the participant a curiosity and a desire to learn new activities. Motivation is also frequently necessary to foster and release the unlimited creative and hidden skills, talents, and powers of the individual or the group. The following suggestions may be useful as motivational devices.

1. Offer opportunities for positive interpersonal relationships that will produce feelings of approval and response from the individual or group.
2. Develop and foster a noncompetitive environment in which all members can find acceptance, support, recognition, and fulfillment.
3. Never involve participants in any activity that will cause them to appear foolish or feel embarrassed.
4. Let the reticent individual sit and observe others enjoying the activity. In most cases the person soon will become actively involved.
5. All program activities should allow for different levels and degrees of participation.
6. Never force an individual into an activity. Such force may cause shy and withdrawn individuals to feel so inadequate and uncomfortable that they may drop out of all activity.
7. Provide activities that build on the strengths and capabilities of the individual and the group.
8. Schedule activities with other age groups in the community. This frequently stimulates interest among mature adults who are reluctant to participate in activities with other older individuals and it may help to rejuvenate other members of the group.
9. Schedule appropriate activities that meet the interest span of the group, obtain the highest degree of participation, help develop wholesome attitudes, fit the time schedule and available facilities, and meet the physical limitations of the individual and the group.
10. Provide an unthreatening, relaxing environment filled with appropriate encouragement and guidance.

11. Encourage participation in a planned, coordinated, structured manner with enjoyable, challenging activities.
12. Patiently listen to what might seem trivial and petty conversation directed toward you. Such warm acceptance can motivate the individual into active participation.

Motivational techniques should be combined with the ability to give sincere and honest praise and encouragement when skills are being mastered or refined. The ability to motivate or channel the interests of the individual and group will be enhanced if the recreator makes a sincere effort to really know and understand all attributes of every mature adult in the program.

The professional recreator should be tactful and skillful in group dynamics and group leadership techniques. Such qualities will enable the recreator to accomplish the following:

1. Provide the necessary framework for involving all participants in group activities
2. Lead and skillfully guide the group
3. Involve all mature adults in accordance with their individual abilities, interests, and talents
4. Assign responsibilities to the various members of the group
5. Motivate individuals within the group to feel responsible for carrying out assigned tasks and responsibilities
6. Direct the group with tact, thus preventing aggressive or outspoken individuals from gaining control and insuring the involvement of shy or withdrawn individuals
7. Make everyone feel a sense of belonging to the group and a vital part of its successful operation
8. Channel the energies of aggressive, authoritative individuals for the benefit of the group
9. Develop within the participants a concern for safety in all activities
10. Establish a noncompetitive atmosphere and maintain an impartial relationship with all members of the group
11. Allow no situation to develop that may arouse jealousies within the group
12. Be aware of and utilize all available community and volunteer resources

The ability to assume responsibility for and carry out the planning, organization, administration, and evaluation of a total social and recreation activity program designed to meet the needs of all mature adults in the group is essential. These skills should include the ability to keep accurate records and reports. In addition, spontaneous flexibility in program planning, organization, and administration, when appropriate, is vital to successful programming. Good human-relations skills also are necessary to establish and maintain a cooperative working relationship with all other professional and volunteer members of the staff and with the clients involved in the program and to assign responsibilities to volunteers and staff directly under the recreator's administration. To insure the type of cooperation needed for conducting a successful program, additional public-relations skills should be directed toward members of the community.

Other skills should include the ability to properly maintain equipment and facilities, the ability to solicit financial assistance in the form of donations and gifts from outside individuals and groups, and the ability to utilize the public-relations media—radio, TV, newspaper—in the community.

Above all, professional recreators working with mature adults must continuously, willingly, and enthusiastically broaden their knowledge, skills, and interests if they are to maintain a high-quality, total recreation program for mature adults. In many situations this includes in-service training, attendance at agency seminars, and attendance at other related professional meetings.

The National Therapeutic Recreation Society, a branch of the National Recreation and Park Association, registers therapeutic-recreation personnel for professional employment at all levels of service, including positions in institutions for the ill and handicapped. The society's policy is to insure that all recreation and patient activity programs, especially in institutions for the ill and handicapped, are directed and supervised by such registered personnel at one of several training levels. Detailed registration information can be obtained from the National Recreation and Park Association, 1601 North Kent Street, Arlington, Virginia 22209.

Proposed standards for therapeutic-recreation personnel working in extended-care facilities and detailed guidelines for therapeutic-recreation service consultants in convalescent hospitals, nursing homes, and mental facilities for the aged are included in detail in the third-quarter, 1970 *Therapeutic Recreation Journal.* The interested student is encouraged to read these materials.

QUALIFICATIONS FOR VOLUNTEERS

Volunteers, or individuals who perform services without financial remuneration, are being used in increasing numbers and in a variety of roles in social and recreational-activity programs for mature adults. In many instances volunteers are college students performing required class fieldwork or internships, high-school students with a sincere desire to help others, or members of religious or other community organizations whose primary function is community service.

Qualified volunteers can be valuable additions to activity programs if they offer talents and skills not possessed by regular staff, foster positive community relationships, increase amount of time available for additional personalized patient contact and attention, and perform routine but necessary trivial tasks.

The type and number of volunteers needed by any organization will be directly related to the size and complexity of the activity program. These volunteer positions can include service volunteers, program-oriented volunteers, advisory volunteers, or administrative volunteers.

Before an organization accepts volunteers, the need for and function of such volunteer services should be determined. Next, written, well-defined and detailed job descriptions should be drawn up for each volunteer position. These job descriptions should include the following:

1. Position title
2. Name of supervisor
3. Time commitment (specific hours where appropriate)
4. Qualifications
5. Required training
6. Specific duties and responsibilities
7. Attire while on duty
8. Required meetings and seminars

After the need for volunteers has been established, local high schools, colleges, and community organizations should be contacted. The acceptable procedures would be to have all volunteers make formal applications and schedule personal interviews.

A standard application form should contain the following:

1. Personal information—name, address, occupation, age, phone number, educational background
2. Check list of skills—arts and crafts, dance, music, social, hobbies, dramatics, clerical, other
3. Leadership experience
4. Past volunteer service
5. Vocational or special training
6. Available time
7. Type of volunteer work desired
8. Availability of transportation—for self and others

The personal interview should be used to assess the following qualifications:

1. Background and experience
2. Skills and talents
3. Motivation for volunteering
4. Emotional maturity
5. Willingness to learn
6. Dependability

During the interview the applicant should be given background information about the organization, including its philosophy and goals or objectives, and detailed information about the job, including all specific functions and duties involved. An applicant who is qualified for the volunteer position should be offered the job.

Before beginning work the volunteer should be oriented to the facilities and staff, including the volunteer's immediate supervisor. This orientation should be followed by all necessary preliminary training needed to properly perform the assigned duties. Frequently, attendance at regularly scheduled seminars at the job site is required for all volunteer staff.

It is advisable to have periodic meetings between volunteers and supervisors to discuss any problems or concerns that may arise regarding any aspects of the volunteer's job.

Evaluation is an important aspect of the total volunteer process. If the volunteer is a college student performing a required internship, the college usually provides the organization with a standardized evaluation form. Or the organization can develop its own form for evaluation purposes. Most standard evaluation forms include a checklist of the following traits to be rated from outstanding to unsatisfactory:

1. Personality—appearance, dress, poise, tact
2. Cooperation—has cordial relations with staff, clients, public
3. Initiative—works effectively without strict supervision
4. Organization—plans and implements program according to needs and objectives
5. Leadership—has well-rounded leadership ability
6. Promotion—submits timely, well-written publicity
7. Dependability—is punctual in carrying out assignments
8. Emotional stability—objectively accepts suggestions and criticism
9. Directed self-development—attends seminars, reads, self-studies
10. Enthusiasm—has interest in work and reflects interest to others
11. Reports—submits reports correctly and promptly
12. Skills—has knowledge and ability in varied activities
13. Safety hazards—recognizes and eliminates them
14. Facility upkeep—maintains bulletin board, play equipment, apparatus, supplies

If, as a result of evaluation, a volunteer is not performing satisfactorily, the person should be told of the weaknesses or shortcomings. After a period of time, if evaluation reports are still unsatisfactory, the volunteer should be released from the job.

Despite the fact that volunteers are unpaid, they should receive personal recognition for the time and effort spent on the job and for the contribution they are making to the total social and recreation activity program. Recognition can take many forms, from a sincere and honest "thank you," to a special certificate of appreciation or special mention on the local bulletin board, to an award for the number of hours worked.

Qualified professional staff and volunteers, combined with total participant involvement in all aspects of the social and recreational activity program, will insure the development and continuation of a valuable program which contributes to the total needs of all mature adults involved.

SELECTED REFERENCES

Hawkins, Donald E., and Verhoven, Peter J. Preparing recreation personnel to provide recreation services to older citizens. *Therapeutic Recreation Journal,* 1970, *3,* (4), 1, 38-43.

Kraus, Richard G., and Bates, Barbara J. *Recreation leadership and supervision: Guidelines for professional development.* Philadelphia: W. B. Saunders, 1975.

Lucus, Carol. *Recreational activity development for the aging in homes, hospitals, and nursing homes.* Springfield, Charles C. Thomas, 1962.

Tague, Jean R. The activity coordinator: An emerging role. *Therapeutic Recreation Journal,* 1974, 7, (3), 114-119.

United States Department of Health, Education and Welfare. *Activities supervisor's guide—A handbook for activities supervisors in long-term care facilities.* Washington, D.C.: DHEW Publication no. (HSM) 73-6706, U.S. Printing Office (reprint), 1972.

Verhoven, Peter J. Recreation and the aging. In *Recreation and Special Populations.* Stein, Thomas A., and Sessoms, H. Douglas. Boston: Holbrook Press, 1973, 379-407.

Vickery, Florence. *How to work with older people—A guide for professional and volunteer leaders of social activity programs for older people.* State of California, Division of Recreation Publication 59-3, 1960.

Writing Committee. Guidelines for the therapeutic recreation service consultant in nursing homes, convalescent hospitals and mental facilities for the aged. *Therapeutic Recreation Journal,* 1970, *3,* (4), 25-35.

9
PROGRAMMING FOR COMMUNITY RECREATION CENTERS, SOCIAL CLUBS, RETIREMENT COMMUNITIES

Age sits with decent grace upon his visage,
And worthily becomes his silver locks;
He bears the marks of many years well spent,
Of virtue truth well tried, and wise experience.
—Rowe

Social clubs, retirement communities, senior centers, and multipurpose senior centers are the most common settings for social and recreational activity programs for mature adults. Although the organizational structure, type of leadership, and purpose of these programs are quite different, they all contain the common element of providing their members with opportunities for recreation, education, and social interaction.

The two largest organizations for older persons in the United States are the American Association of Retired Persons and the National Council of Senior Citizens. In addition to the regular membership benefits, these organizations may sponsor local social programs for their members. The American Association of Retired Persons, founded in 1958 and open to all persons 55 years of age or over, for example, provides its members with the following benefits:

1. Bimonthly publications (each on an alternate month)
    a. *Modern Maturity,* a magazine containing information on health, food, travel, sports, books, legislation, and miscellaneous activities
    b. *AARP News Bulletin,* a newsletter containing informative news of national developments, local association activities, and additional information of practical value to the reader

2. Low, money-saving prices on vitamins, prescriptions, drugs, medical appliances, sickroom supplies, and health aids delivered by mail
3. Counseling service on preparation for retirement
4. Group health insurance to supplement Medicare
5. Group automobile insurance, guaranteed renewable and noncancelable up to age 80
6. Hospitality houses and lounges in St. Petersburg, Florida, Long Beach, California, and Washington, D.C., to provide visiting members with information on local services and events
7. Low-cost group travel programs for trips in the United States and abroad
8. Lifetime learning institutes in Washington, D.C., and Long Beach, California, in addition to a Wednesday-morning lecture series featured on many radio stations
9. Legislative programs to alert and inform its members on issues of concern to all older persons on fixed incomes

SOCIAL CLUBS

Social clubs are frequently organized for a specific purpose, such as a travel club, gardening club, homemakers club, nature club, birdwatchers club, ecology club, and bridge club. These are usually composed of local groups of mature adults who organize because of some common interest they wish to share.

The Golden Age or XYZ Clubs have existed across the nation since 1947. These clubs are usually sponsored by the local recreation department or public-school division of adult education. They are primarily social or recreational in nature, meeting only once or twice weekly and usually having volunteer or nonprofessional leadership. The big single difference between the two groups is that the Golden Age Club is open to men and women, whereas XYZ Club membership is restricted to men only. A typical meeting consists of informal visiting, a community sing, introduction of guests, announcements of birthdays and anniversaries, and presentation of new members. A business meeting is usually followed by a social hour of cards or games, or a special program of music, skits, a movie, or a speaker. Simple refreshments generally conclude the meeting. No membership fees are assessed. Voluntary contributions, however, are accepted to pay for refreshments, purchase of birthday and special greeting cards, and to defray other miscellaneous expenses.

Golden-Age and XYZ-Club programs frequently include bowling, swimming, and gymnasium activities; birthday parties; occasional bus trips throughout the local state; dances; annual craft fairs; annual picnics; annual recognition programs for members who gave voluntary service to the community during the year; and musical variety shows performed by members.

Frequently, religious organizations sponsor Golden Age Clubs. One such example is the Catholic Golden Age Club, a national organization established in 1973 for members of the Catholic faith over 50 years of age. Its purpose is to help members lead more secure, comfortable, and pleasurable lives. Annual dues are two dollars, or a three-year membership can be purchased for five dollars.

National membership in the Catholic Golden Age Club includes the following benefits:

1. A subscription to the *Catholic Golden Age Newsletter* which includes consumer tips, travel-plan information, news of upcoming member benefits, nutrition information, and spiritual writings
2. Discounts up to 25 percent or guaranteed rates at national hotel and motel chains
3. Group travel packages at budget prices to select locations in the United States and foreign countries
4. Discounts, through national pharmaceutical suppliers, up to 40 percent on vitamins, prescriptions, and medications and up to 76 percent on generic equivalents
5. Discounts on eyeglasses
6. Low-cost photo processing
7. Reduced group-rate life and health insurance, regardless of health, to supplement Medicare and other health insurance
8. 20 percent discount on rental cars
9. Discount prices on best-selling books and novels, including religious books and other articles,
10. Spiritual benefits

At the local level Catholic Golden Age Clubs offer members retreats, sociability and new friendships, field trips to area points of interest, special bus tours with knowledgeable guides, guest speakers, educational programs geared to local group interests, and consumer advocacy.

RETIREMENT COMMUNITIES

Retirement, or adult, communities are specially planned and constructed villages for affluent and usually highly educated elderly. Most residents of such communities are vibrant, happy, carefree people who have thrown all their cares aside to enjoy their retirement years. The homes in these villages are functionally geared to the needs of this segment of our population and frequently contain special safety and security features, including high walls and guards to keep intruders out of the entire community. Additional services such as community housekeeping, property and yard maintenance, and meals may be included as a part of the costs. Many of these villages have elaborate recreational facilities such as golf courses, swimming pools, and tennis courts. Social and recreational activity programs are common features of retirement communities. These programs are usually organized by a paid professional director in cooperation with members of the village, who act as a council to make policies and help carry out the diverse program of activities.

COMMUNITY RECREATION CENTERS

There are several common types of community-based recreation centers for senior citizens. These centers may be sponsored by the municipal recreation and park department, public or private agencies (including religious federations), or public housing or welfare agencies. As with social-club and retirement-village programs, they provide their members with opportunities for recreation, education, and social interaction.

The two most common community-recreation centers for mature adults are senior centers and multipurpose senior centers. Both function under the guidance of professional leadership, have their own facilities, and meet for substantial periods of time daily, or several days per week, including weekends. Multipurpose senior centers usually meet daily and offer a wider variety of health and social services than senior centers.

Typical programs at senior centers include informal visiting; professionally directed crafts, hobbies, and group activities; a wide variety of social activities; sports and games; instructional classes; counseling services; musical activities; physical conditioning; weight-watching programs; special trips and outings; special newspapers; library services; tournaments; and seminars related to consumer protection, dental care, fraud schemes, and housing.

Multipurpose senior centers are usually established with a broad-based sponsorship of several diverse and influential groups. An ideal sponsorship combination includes three major forms of organizations and groups.

1. A public department
   a. Local or state recreation and parks department
   b. Local or state department of health
   c. Local education department
   d. Mayor's office
2. A private social-welfare agency
   a. Settlement or neighborhood center
   b. Jewish Community Center
   c. YMCA or YWCA
   d. Salvation Army
   e. Organizations for the blind

     f.   Family service agencies
     g,   Volunteers of America
     h.   Hearing societies
     i.   Homes and hospitals for the aging
3.   A volunteer citizens' community, club, or group
     a.   National Council for Jewish Women
     b.   Junior Leagues of America
     c.   Altrusa clubs
     d.   Soroptomists
     e.   Rotary
     f.   Kiwanis
     g.   Local foundations
     h.   Councils on aging
     i.   Community groups or clubs
     j.   Religious organizations
     k.   Labor unions
     l.   Corporations

The responsibilities of sponsorship of a multipurpose senior center include:

1.   To act as an adjunct to the professional staff by providing the type of dynamic leadership needed to inspire the community's confidence in and support of the center's operation and growth. The sponsors do not operate the center.
2.   To provide financial assistance by developing adequate budgets and fund-raising plans and by assuming the responsibility for seeing that all center expenditures are met.
3.   To provide consultation regarding operational policies.
4.   To provide for or assist with physical plant operations and other program equipment and needs.
5.   To assure the continuous operation of the center.
6.   To aid in the recruitment of volunteers.
7.   To stimulate cordial relationships with all elements of the community.
8.   To interpret the meaning and value of the center's purpose and function to potential members and other segments of the community.
9.   To appoint responsible and dedicated representatives to the center's board of directors and advisory committee.

    The National Institute of Senior Centers (The National Council on the Aging, Inc.), founded in March of 1970, serves as a central resource to help develop, improve, and expand the services and programs of senior centers throughout the country by providing a broad range of services and expert technical assistance for planning and programming.

1.   Collection, preparation, and circulation of information on all aspects of center operation

2. Consultant services to currently established centers and to communities desiring to establish such centers
3. Formation of operating standards for centers
4. Establishment of regional and national conferences and seminars
5. Assistance to center personnel through a national clearing-house program
6. Cooperation with national organizations and governmental agencies at all levels
7. Stimulation of research projects to improve center service
8. Encouragement of student training for work with the aging

Typical Goals of Multipurpose Senior Centers

Multipurpose senior centers should establish the following goals:

1. To provide mature adults with the opportunity for meaningful and satisfying group and individual relationships designed to fulfill many of their social, physical, and intellectual needs.
2. To help mature adults learn new skills of enrichment and self-expression and to expand their interests, tap their potential, and develop their talents in the arts, music, drama, nature, language, current events, dance, crafts, games, trips and camping, and similar activities.
3. To provide members with opportunities for demonstrating their performance talents.
4. To offer opportunities for mature adults to be useful and to provide service to others through volunteer action programs. (See chapter 4, Sociological Aspects of Aging, for a description of these programs.)
   a. Link the senior community to the community at large and help mature adults become an integral part of the community.
   b. Help seniors assume a valued role in the society and gain a strengthened self-concept.
   c. Dispel the inaccurate stereotype of the inactive older person.
5. To assist mature adults in maintaining good physical health.
   a. Programs conducted in physical fitness.
   b. Nutritional, low-cost meals in a social setting.
   c. Educational programs on wise food planning and purchasing.
   d. Medical and dental care.
   e. General health programs, including special activities for individuals with limited vision, hearing loss, and other physical limitations.
6. To promote the mental health of mature adults.
   a. Use and development of their creative abilities.
   b. Exposure to a healthy social environment that counteracts social isolation.
   c. Provision of counseling services where needed.

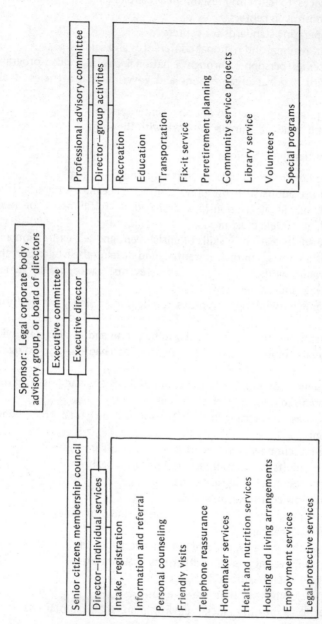

Model organization chart for multipurpose senior center

Recommended by National Council on Aging

7. To help the mature adult keep informed about changes in the community and the world.
   a.   Organized discussion groups and scheduled speakers to stimulate interest in current issues.
   b.   Classes in language skills and various occupations to stimulate community involvement.
   c.   Leadership training and group awareness programs to encourage greater social involvement of the participants.
8. To facilitate active participation by mature adults in programs and organizations serving older persons.
9. To give mature adults the opportunity to assume leadership roles.
10. To strengthen the personal effectiveness of mature adults in working with others.
11. To offer mature adults counseling and referral service, guidance and assistance, where necessary, in personal and legal-service areas such as health, housing, Social Security, safety, legal aid, family, and finances.
12. To provide vital services and offer a wide range of vocational and recreational activities to mature adults in a conducive, noncompetitive atmosphere. This includes a balanced, meaningful, and enjoyable program of individual and group services.
13. To encourage the development of part-time and full-time employment for mature adults through community resources. Cooperatives formed by many centers provide sources of additional income for members.
14. To provide services for the homebound. Frequently, center members serve as friendly visitors and shopping aides, maintain regular phone contact, offer minor home repairs, and deliver nutritious meals to the homebound mature adult.
15. To provide members with transportation by special vehicles to libraries, museums, doctors' offices, grocery stores, and shopping centers that are difficult to reach by public transportation and are too expensive to reach by taxi or private limousine.
16. To provide opportunity for mature adults to perform social service as volunteers in hospitals, homes for the aged, children's institutions, schools, and national service organizations.

Facilities and Equipment

Although any facilities that meet minimum standards of health and safety will suffice for social and recreational-activity programs for mature adults, the following factors will make the facilities more desirable:
1. Central location where the greatest concentration of mature adults reside. If the potential users of the facility are spread out in a large metropolitan

area, many small centers may be more practical than one large center.

2. Accessibility via main roads and public transportation for those individuals not within walking distance of the center. In many cities bus companies provide reduced rates for this segment of the population. If bus use is great enough, companies may be willing to set up alternate bus routes during the hours when mature adults will be going to and returning from the center. Where no public transportation is available, some communities utilize school buses during off-hours to transport mature adults to and from scheduled activities.

3. Easy accessibility from the street. Handrails on steps, which should not be too steep, ramps and other architectural features for convenient use by individuals in wheelchairs or with other limitations are desirable. If programs are conducted after dark, stairs should be well lighted.

4. Activities confined to one floor of a building. There are several advantages to such an arrangement:
   a. Activities are easily accessible to those individuals with physical limitations who cannot climb stairs.
   b. Programming is facilitated by the fact that it is easier to expose participants to a variety of activities. Such exposure can be motivational and increase participation.
   c. Leadership and supervision problems are reduced.

5. A variety of rooms that are well lighted and ventilated with properly controlled air conditioning and heating.
   a. Small multipurpose meeting rooms for classes and other instructional sessions.
   b. Craft shops.
   c. Health maintenance offices.
   d. Large room which can be used as a combination auditorium, social hall, and dining hall.
   e. Library.
   f. Lounge.
   g. Administrative offices.
   h. Restrooms that are well lighted, conveniently located, and accessible to individuals with physical limitations.
   i. Kitchen for preparing refreshments and providing other limited food service.
   j. Storage areas, including cabinets, for all large and small equipment and supplies. If facilities are used by other groups, storage areas should have locks.

6. Minimum equipment should include tables, chairs, dishes, a piano, record player, movie projector, sewing machine, mimeograph machine, and typewriter.
7. Supplies should include games, crafts, first-aid materials, and program supplies determined by the program content.

Finances

Both the type of activity program offered and the type of program sponsorship will determine the amount of money needed to finance the program and the typical sources available for such funds. The common needs for funds include monies to rent or renovate facilities, to purchase equipment and supplies, and to pay salaries of staff.

Costs can be reduced if existing recreation facilities are used, especially if the program is sponsored by the local public recreation and park department. Frequently, local churches open their facilities and do not charge rental fees to mature adults who are members of the congregation. Many other sponsoring agencies follow this same procedure, especially when they are recipients of public or voluntary funds.

When funds are needed, the group can hold such money-making events as bazaars, play productions, and concerts. Flexible membership fees, based on the participant's ability to pay, can be assessed. Contributions can be solicited from individuals or organizations in the community.

Publicity regarding the program, which stresses its interrelatedness to other community activities, can facilitate community contributions. This can also open the door for team fund-raising efforts with other community service personnel.

Activity Selection and Scheduling

Before setting up a schedule of activities for inclusion in the program, some type of needs-and-interests survey should be completed by the participants. An all-inclusive Suggested Interest Inventory appears on the next several pages. This form can and should be shortened or refined by the recreation director, based on the type and quantity of available supplies and facilities, including provision for any necessary multischeduling of other groups and leadership talents of the professional and volunteer recreation staff. (See chapter 6, Sports and Exercise, for suggested guidelines.)

If a facility is shared by several groups, frequently the activity program for mature adults can be scheduled during the hours when children are in school and other adults are at work. Common scheduling hours are from 9 A.M. to 5 P.M. with occasional evening programs from 7 P.M. to 10 or 11 P.M.

Schedules should be planned at least one month in advance, duplicated, distributed to members, and posted on the bulletin board. Additional weekly reminders of special activities are also beneficial. A sample activity schedule appears immediately after the Suggested Interest Inventory in this chapter.

When special events are planned on a local, city, or district basis, the following guidelines should be observed:

1. Make all necessary preliminary plans and reservations with administrative personnel, including date, transportation, facilities, equipment, and time schedule.
2. Encourage mature adults to assist with all aspects of planning, preparation, and leadership.
3. Arrange for staff and volunteer coverage of activities well in advance of the date.
4. Assign specific duties to staff and volunteers assisting with all aspects of the program.
5. Make all necessary arrangements with the housekeeping staff if center facilities are to be used and special equipment or facilities need to be set up.
6. Arrange with dietary staff for refreshments.
7. When appropriate, check with medical personnel or available medical records to determine the type of activities for inclusion in the program.
8. Make arrangements for someone to record all aspects of the special events on film for later display.

SUGGESTED INTEREST INVENTORY

Name:_____

Please check the activities you would enjoy and would like to have included in the social and recreation activity program.

Games and Sports

* indicates that the activity can be modified or adapted for extended-care facilities.

__ Aerobic dance	__ Bowling*
__ Archery	__ Box hockey
__ Badminton	__ Bridge*
__ Balloon volleyball*	__ Bumper pool*
__ Basketball (modified)	__ Bunco*
__ Bean bag toss*	__ Camping
__ Billiards*	__ Cards*
__ Bingo*	__ Casting*
__ Boating*	__ Checkers*

— Chess*
— Chinese checkers*
— Cribbage*
— Croquet*
— Cycling
— Dancing (folk, social, square)*
— Darts*
— Deck tennis*
— Dominoes*
— Fishing*
— Games (table, active, guessing)*
— Golf
— Group exercises*
— Hearts*
— Horseshoes*
— Ice skating
— Jogging
— Miniature golf*
— Monopoly*
— Nature hikes*
— Paddle tennis
— Parchesi*
— Handball
— Other:_____

— Physical fitness activities*
— Pinochle*
— Pokeno*
— Pool*
— Puzzles*
— Quoits*
— Relays
— Rifle/shotgun shooting
— Ring toss*
— Roller skating
— Rummy*
— Scrabble*
— Shuffleboard*
— Skiing (Alpine and Nordic)
— Snowshoeing
— Softball
— Solitaire*
— Squash racquets
— Swimming*
— Table tennis
— Tennis
— Volleyball
— Walking

Arts and Crafts

— Basketry*
— Birdfeeder construction*
— Block printing
— Bookbinding and repair
— Braid weaving*
— Candlemaking
— Carpentry
— Carving (soap and wood)*
— Ceramics
— Chenille crafts*
— Clay and plastercraft
— Colonial mat making*
— Cooking*
— Copper enameling
— Copper tooling

— Cork craft*
— Crocheting*
— Decoupage
— Drawing*
— Embroidery*
— Flower arranging*
— Flower making*
— Fly tying*
— Furniture refinishing
— Gardening*
— Graphic arts (printing)
— Hairpin lace*
— Hooked rugs*
— Knitting*
— Knotting*

__ Leathercraft*
__ Liquid embroidery*
__ Loop weaving*
__ Macaroni craft*
__ Macrame*
__ Matchbook decoration*
__ Metalcraft
__ Millinery
__ Mosaics (tile, seed, gravel)*
__ Naturecraft*
__ Needlecraft*
__ Painting (tempera, oil, water)*
__ Papercraft*
__ Photography*
__ Pipe cleaner animals*
__ Pom pom rugs*
__ Puppetry*
__ Quilting*
__ Rake knitting*
__ Rug making*
__ Sculpture*

__ Sewing*
__ Shellcraft*
__ Soap sculpture and painting*
__ Sponge craft*
__ Stenciling*
__ Swedish weaving*
__ Tatting*
__ Textile painting*
__ Toy making (cloth, wood)*
__ Toy repairing
__ Turkish knotting*
__ Video-tape production
__ Weaving*
__ Whittling*
__ Woodcarving
__ Woodworking
__ Writing (newsletter, prose, poetry)*
__ Yarn animals and dolls*
__ Other:_____

Discussion Groups

__ Bible study*
__ Book reviews*
__ Community resources for
__ older citizens
__ Conservation of sight, hearing*
__ Current events*
__ Debates*
__ House plants and their care*

__ Investments*
__ Politics*
__ Social Security*
__ Sports*
__ State and federal legislation
__ related to older citizens*
__ Wills and legal affairs*
__ Other:_____

Trips

__ Amusement complexes
__ Beaches
__ Boat trips*
__ Church services*
__ Concerts
__ Dramatic events
__ Movies
__ Musical events
__ Other:_____

__ Parks
__ Picnics*
__ Plays
__ Political rallies
__ Scenic locations
__ Sightseeing
__ Sport events
__ Zoos

Miscellaneous

— Auctions and craft sales
— Band*
— Bird watching*
— Center newspaper*
— Chorus*
— Clubs:*
  — Book
  — Camera
  — Choral
  — Garden
  — History
  — Language
  — Other:_____
— Collecting:
  — Coins
  — Rocks
  — Stamps
  — Other:_____
— Community service:*
  — Assist public agencies
  — Visit homebound
  — Visit hospitals
  — Other:_____
— Community singing*
— Other:_____

— Entertainment by performing
  groups*
— Music listening*
— Open house
— Parties:*
  — Birthday
  — Holiday
  — Potluck dinners
  — Other:_____
— Publishing newspaper*
— Quizzes*
— Radio listening*
— Rhythm band*
— Slide shows*
— Small instrument group*
— Story telling*
— Television*
— Visiting speakers*
— Volunteer work:*
  — Blind
  — Handicapped
  — Homebound
  — Other:_____
— Writing classes

Please list your specific talents that you would like to share with the group, including interest in teaching skills, directing musicals, *et cetera*.

_____
_____
_____
_____
_____

BASIC PROGRAMMING PRINCIPLES

If an effective, functional social and recreational activity program is to be developed and implemented for mature adults, the following basic programming principles should be observed:

1. Offer programs near the homes and immediate neighborhoods where the bulk of the older population reside.

SAMPLE MONTHLY ACTIVITY SCHEDULE

Sunday	Monday	Tuesday	Wednesday	Thursday	Friday	Saturday
	1 10 A.M. Bible class Catholic Protestant 1 P.M. Choral group 3 P.M. Kitchen band 4 P.M. Exercise 7 P.M. Dancing (Square and folk)	2 10 A.M. Art class, Wood work, Quilting 1 P.M. Leather class, Drama 3 P.M. Exercise	3 12 noon Covered dish luncheon Guest speaker 2 P.M. Informal activity	4 10 A.M. Bowling 1 P.M. Culinary arts 3 P.M. Crafts	5 10 A.M. Games 1 P.M. Crafts 3 P.M. Exercise 7 P.M. Bingo	6 10 A.M. Exercise 11 A.M. Crafts 1 P.M. Informal activity 7 P.M. Social dance
7 1–5 P.M. Informal activity	8 10 A.M. Bible class Catholic Protestant 1 P.M. Choral group 3 P.M. Kitchen band 4 P.M. Exercise 7 P.M. Square dancing	9 10 A.M. Art class, Wood work, Quilting 1 P.M. Leather class, Drama 3 P.M. Exercise	10 12 noon Covered dish luncheon Guest speaker 2 P.M. Informal activity	11 10 A.M. Bowling 1 P.M. Culinary arts 3 P.M. Crafts	12 10 A.M. Games 1 P.M. Crafts 3 P.M. Exercise 7 P.M. Bingo	13 10 A.M. Exercise 11 A.M. Crafts 1 P.M. Informal activity 7 P.M. Hamlet (Reservations required)
14 1–5 P.M. Variety show, refreshments	15 10 A.M. Bible class Catholic Protestant 1 P.M. Choral group 3 P.M. Kitchen band 4 P.M. Exercise 7 P.M. Folk dancing	16 10 A.M. Art class, Wood work, Quilting 1 P.M. Leather class, Drama 3 P.M. Exercise	17 12 noon Covered dish luncheon Guest speaker 2 P.M. Informal activity	18 10 A.M. Bowling 1 P.M. Culinary arts 3 P.M. Crafts	19 10 A.M. Games 1 P.M. Crafts 3 P.M. Exercise 7 P.M. Bingo	20 10 A.M. Exercise 11 A.M. Crafts 1 P.M. Informal activity 7 P.M. Symphony (Reservations required)
21 1–5 P.M. Informal activity	22 10 A.M. Bible class Catholic Protestant 1 P.M. Choral group 3 P.M. Kitchen band 7 P.M. Square dance	23 10 A.M. Art class, Wood work, Quilting 1 P.M. Leather class, Drama 3 P.M. Exercise	24 7 A.M. Trip to Kentucky Lake (Reservations required)	25 10 A.M. Bowling 1 P.M. Culinary arts 3 P.M. Crafts	26 10 A.M. Games 1 P.M. Crafts 3 P.M. Exercise 7 P.M. Bingo	27 10 A.M. Exercise 11 A.M. Crafts 1 P.M. Informal activity 7 P.M. Ballet (Reservations required)
28 1–5 P.M. Informal activity	29 10 A.M. Bible class Catholic Protestant 1 P.M. Choral group 3 P.M. Kitchen band 4 P.M. Exercise 7 P.M. Folk dance	30 10 A.M. Art class, Wood work, Quilting 1 P.M. Leather class, Drama 3 P.M. Exercise	31 10 A.M. Bowling tournament 7 P.M. Bowling awards banquet			

2. Involve mature adults in all aspects of program planning. Remember that only when mature adults, themselves, participate in the planning, do the social and recreational activities become more meaningful to them. By participating in the actual program planning, mature adults evidence their own dignity and independence and increase their feelings of importance to themselves and others. Such leadership and involvement can contribute markedly to the program, especially when the mature adult shares talents and skills with others in the group.

3. Offer a diverse program of activities, keeping in mind the fact that what may be diversion for one individual may be hard work for another.
   a. Meet needs of the group, based on their past opportunities and experiences.
       (1) Educational background and value systems of low-income groups.
       (2) Higher-income groups with more educational, cultural, and social advantages.
   b. Do not overemphasize one type of activity to the detriment of others.
   c. Keep competition friendly; do not allow it to grow into an unhealthy competitive situation, as may occur especially in card games.
   d. Add variety and interest to the program by capitalizing on the backgrounds of the members and recognizing their various customs, traditions, and religious holidays.
   e. Create goals and purposes for learning and doing; activity for activity's sake is not meaningful. Therefore, include meaningful and useful activities in the program.
       (1) Work on projects that are useable or sellable.
       (2) Develop skills to put on a production such as a glee club.
       (3) Accept orders to make items for other groups.
   f. The activity program should be flexible to permit individuals to move from one activity to another.
       (1) Helps stimulate interest in new activities.
       (2) Arouses curiosity about activities.
       (3) See chapter 8, Staff—Professional and Volunteer, for motivational devices.

4. Prevent the program from becoming so static that it meets resistance from the group. This can be avoided if all members are involved in the program planning, and if plans are not made too far in advance. Activities should not be scheduled more than a month in advance.

5. Keep the program-planning process continuous and ongoing.

6. Minimize or eliminate all possible situations that may cause embarrassment to any of the members of the group:

    a. Avoid placing an individual in situations where that person may be unable to continue participation due to the very nature of the activity, such as excessive physical exertion, or eye strain.

    b. Avoid time restraints for the completion of an activity.

    c. Provide sufficient funds to purchase materials necessary to complete a project.

    d. Avoid placing an overly self-conscious individual in front of a group to perform unwillingly.

7. Plan activities with other age groups, whenever possible. Skill, interest, and talent, not age, should be the criteria used in this type of programming.

8. Make the atmosphere of the social and recreational activity program conducive to the development of such positive relationships as cooperation, growth in understanding and acceptance of others, and the relinquishment of selfish attitudes. A program is more than activities; it also includes the individual and group relationships and interactions which take place during participation.

9. Make special efforts to reach the economically deprived, isolated, and ill and handicapped mature adults living in the community. Team your efforts with other community service personnel to facilitate this goal.

10. Include service projects in the program. Such activity satisfies the individual's need to be a useful member of society. In addition to the service projects listed in chapter 4, Sociological Aspects of Aging, opportunities in the community for such service might include:

    a. Visiting the sick or homebound aged or handicapped.

    b. Reading to the blind or partially sighted.

    c. Teaching English to the foreign born.

    d. Assisting with fund-raising projects for other community health and welfare organizations.

11. Add variety and stimulation to the program by planning trips and excursions. Such activity can include scenic, historical, and cultural trips designed to broaden interests and stimulate thinking of all members involved in the activity. Trips and excursions should be well planned and organized several weeks before the scheduled date and supervised by a responsible guide.

12. Provide food and refreshments to add desirable social and emotional overtones to the program and to contribute to the nutritional needs of the members of the group.

13. Produce a monthly or weekly newspaper containing schedule information and other items of interest regarding all aspects of the program and its participants. This can stimulate interest in the program and motivate the participants, especially if their involvement provides them with the opportunity to get their names and activity participation into the newspaper.

PROGRAM RECORDS

Accurate, detailed, and ongoing records should be kept on all recreation programs for mature adults. Such records facilitate program evaluation and justify needed increases in staff, equipment, supplies, and facilities.

Although the size and complexity of the recreation program and the characteristics of the population served frequently determine the specific kind and number of records kept, typical program records should include the participants' registration forms, attendance records, the monthly calendar of events, and the volunteer records.

Participant Registration Form

To insure the participant's right to privacy, these records should be kept confidential. The form should be devised to obtain accurate data regarding the participant's needs, interests, abilities, and disabilities. Accurate participant-registration forms can be extremely valuable in facilitating effective program planning. The form should include the following minimum information:

1. Background information—name, address, telephone number, age, ethnic background
2. Present leisure interests
3. Talents that can be shared with the group
4. Potential medical limitations
5. Person to contact in case of an emergency

Attendance Records

These records facilitate program evaluation and program planning. In addition, they justify requests for additional program monies, facilities, staff, and supplies. Attendance records should be kept on all organized and spontaneous individual and group activities, including special events. These records should contain the following information:

1. Frequency of participation
2. Type of participation—active vs. passive
3. Quality of participation
4. Length of participation

Monthly Calendar of Events

These records give a clear and concise overview of the total monthly program. In addition, they facilitate the long-range planning of facilities, equipment, staff, and volunteers. A monthly calendar of events serves as an excellent cross-check with attendance records in program planning. The monthly calendar should include the following data:

1. Date, time, and location of all scheduled events

2. Deadline dates for reservations for special events
3. Open hours for free, spontaneous activity

Volunteer Records

To insure the volunteer's right to privacy, these records should be kept confidential. These records will be beneficial to justify the need for additional staff and are essential as a reference for filling in recommendations based on a volunteer's effective on-the-job performance. These records should be accurate and complete, and should include these items:

1. Time on the job—hours by day, week, month
2. Quality of performance
3. Interpersonal relationships
4. Initiative

See chapter 8, Qualifications for Volunteers, for additional information.

PROGRAM EVALUATION

If social and recreational activity programs for mature adults are to be successful, the program-planning process must be continuous and ongoing; it must be based on an effective, honest, thorough, and systematic evaluation system. The records outlined in the preceding material can and should be an integral part of this evaluation process.

Because the primary purpose of evaluation is to determine the effectiveness of the program of activities in relation to program goals, it should be a continuous process. Depending on the type of evaluation undertaken, it can occur daily, weekly, bimonthly, monthly, semiannually, annually, or in various combinations. In most situations certain aspects of the program are evaluated more frequently than others. As an example, special hospitals and institutions may evaluate individual participation daily, community support and involvement monthly, and public and private support biannually. The frequency of evaluation should be directly related to the specific goals and objectives of the program. Regardless of the frequency of the evaluation process, results should be used as a means of improving the quality of the social and recreational activity program for mature adults.

Items most frequently included in the evaluation process are the following:

1. The individual participant
   a. Frequency of attendance
   b. Degree of involvement
   c. Nature of participation
   d. Ability to function effectively in both individual and group situations, including cooperation

    e. Attitudinal changes, including strengthening of self-concept
    f. Changes in acceptance of responsibility
2. The activity program
    a. Diversity of activities to meet all needs
       (1) Both sexes
       (2) Varied socioeconomic groups
       (3) Varied needs and interests of all participants
    b. Appropriateness of scheduling for needs of group
    c. Appropriateness of activities to stimulate participation
    d. Adequacy of program promotional techniques
    e. Initiative and imagination of staff and volunteers in the programming process
    f. Effectiveness of program in enriching the leisure life of the participants
    g. Success in reaching or achieving specific program goals and objectives
3. The community
    a. Interest and support of program by members of the community
       (1) Cooperative efforts with other groups in the community
       (2) Volunteers from the community
       (3) Special projects sponsored by the community
    b. Favorable public support through news media

An effective social and recreational activity program for mature adults can evolve if cooperative efforts of the participants, staff, and volunteers are supplemented with sound programming principles refined by an ongoing evaluation process. The combined results will be ample evidence of the value of such mutual efforts.

SELECTED REFERENCES

Anderson, Nancy N. *Senior centers: Information from a national survey.* Minneapolis: American Rehabilitation Foundation, 1969.

Avedon, Elliott M. Aging apprehension, and antipathy. In *Recreation issues and perspectives,* eds. Herbert Brantley and H. Douglas Sessoms. Columbia, S.C.: Wing Publications, 1969, 114-119.

Avedon, Elliott M. A new leisure and older people: Implications for therapeutic recreation service. *Therapeutic Recreation Journal,* 1970, *3,* (4), 3-8, 24.

Bashaw, Mary E. Cincinnati's community action therapeutic recreation project for the aged. *Therapeutic Recreation Journal,* 1968, *3,* (2), 16-19.

Bultena, Gordon, and Wood, Vivian. Leisure orientation and recreational activities of retirement community residents. *Journal of Leisure Research,* Winter 1970, *2,* 3-16.

Consiglio, Eileen E. Leisure and senior citizens: A new complexity. *Leisurability,* 1976, *3,* (1), 21-28.

Cross, Gertrude. *Program ideas for senior citizens.* Flint, Mich.: Advertisers Press, 1970.

Dlizbe, Wilma. Why recreation programs for the aging. *Recreation,* 1955, 2, 48.

Halberg, Kathleen J. Individualized planning for the aging resident. In *Expanding horizons in therapeutic recreation II,* ed. Jerry D. Kelley, 1974, 105-109.

Hayes, Gene A. A case study of municipal recreation programs for senior citizens and the handicapped. *Therapeutic Recreation Journal,* 1972, 6, (1), 2, 34.

Hayes, Gene A. Recreation and leisure: Implications for the aged. *Therapeutic Recreation Journal,* 1974, 8, (3), 138-144.

Kaplan, Jerome. Functions and objectives of a senior citizens' center. *Geriatrics,* 1962, 17, 771-777.

Lucas, Carol. *Recreation in gerontology.* Springfield, Ill.: Charles C. Thomas, 1964.

Maser, Kemp A. Recreation in a retirement village. *Recreation in Treatment Centers,* 1965, 4, 13-15.

Maynard, Marianne. Achieving emotional well-being for the aged through leisure programs. *Therapeutic Recreation Journal,* 1974, 8, (2), 64-67.

Merryman, Elizabeth L. Warmth in the golden years. *Journal of Health, Physical Education, and Recreation,* 1973, 11, 44-45.

Mullen, Dorothy G. Recreation for the aging. In *Expanding horizons in therapeutic recreation II,* ed. Jerry D. Kelly, 1974, 21-28.

Nash, Bernard E. Retirement as leisure. *Journal of Health, Physical Education, and Recreation,* 1972, 3, 50.

Newsweek. Can aging be cured? April 16, 1973, 56-66.

Pierce, C. H. Recreation for the elderly: Activity participation at a senior citizen center. *The Gerontologist,* 1975, 15, (3), 202-205.

Sessoms, H. Douglas. *Aging: Its physiological, recreational and health implications.* Lafayette, Ind.: Purdue University Press, 1969.

Shelton, Rudolph H. Recreation for the handicapped and aging: The need in Westchester County, New York. *Therapeutic Recreation Journal,* 1968, 2, (3), 9-13.

Stein, Thomas A. The need and approach to recreation services with older persons. *Therapeutic Recreation Journal,* 1968, 2, (2), 3-10.

Time. New outlook for the aged. June 2, 1975, 44-49.

Verhoven, Peter J. Recreation and the aging. In *Recreation and special populations,* eds. H. D. Sessoms and T. A. Stein, Boston: Holbrook Press, 1973.

Vickery, Florence E. *Creative programming for older adults: A leadership training guide.* New York: Association Press, 1972.

Weiss, Caroline R. Learning and planning for retirement. *Journal of Health, Physical Education, and Recreation,* 1976, 3, 51-52.

Williams, Arthur. *Recreation for the aging.* New York: Association Press, 1953.

Williams, Arthur. *Recreation in the senior years.* New York: Association Press, 1962.

10
PROGRAMMING FOR EXTENDED-CARE FACILITIES

He is miserable and wretched
And Ignorant too,
Who has nothing to do,
When he has nothing to do.

He is rich and happy,
And fortunate too,
Who has plenty to do,
When he has nothing to do.
—O. O. Arnold

Although many of the programming principles included in the preceding chapter can be adapted to extended-care facilities, in most cases special programming considerations are essential to insure maximum participation by all residents, both ambulatory and bedfast, or nonambulatory.

The 1970 amendments of the Older Americans' Act mandate that extended-care facilities receiving Medicare and Medicaid benefits provide activity programs for their patients. In January of 1974 new Federal rules and regulations were issued for the operation of skilled nursing homes. The following section of these rules and regulations relates to activity programs in these facilities (United States Department of Health, Education, and Welfare, January 17, 1974, 405.1131):

> *Condition of Participation—Patient Activities. The skilled nursing facility provides for an activities program, appropriate to the needs and interests of each patient, to encourage self care, resumption of*

167

normal activities, and maintenance of an optimal level of psychosocial functioning.

a.   Standard: Responsibility for Patient Activities. A member of the facility's staff is designated as responsible for the patient activities program. If he is not a qualified patient activities coordinator, he functions with frequent, regularly scheduled consultation from a person so qualified.

b.   Standard: Patient Activities Program. Provision is made for an ongoing program of meaningful activities appropriate to the needs and interests of patients, designed to promote opportunities for engaging in normal pursuits, including religious activities of their choice, if any. Each patient's activities program is approved by the patient's attending physician as not in conflict with the treatment plan. The activities are designed to promote the physical, social, and mental well-being of the patients. The facility makes available adequate space and a variety of supplies and equipment to satisfy the individual interests of patients.

The recreator employed in a nursing home is encouraged to read these rules and regulations for a detailed interpretation of the legal requirements for operating a nursing facility.

It is important to note that Federal rules and regulations do not automatically insure the inclusion of regularly scheduled activity programs in nursing homes. In a recent trip to a nursing home to visit a friend, I was surrounded by inactivity. In fact, the posted activity schedule was two months old! Such situations are still all too common in extended-care facilities across the country. Sincere efforts of concerned professional and community individuals are necessary if the desired programming changes are to occur in these facilities.

Top-quality, daily recreation programs suited to the unique needs, interests, and abilities of each and every resident should be the goal of all personnel employed in extended-care facilities. Programs should be diverse and include active and passive programs of individual and group activities of a social, physical, and creative nature.

An activity program in an extended-care facility should be more than recreation. It is everything that happens to a resident—all the interactions in which he is engaged. An activity program means the conscious management of daily life through creating, supporting, developing, and restoring the appropriate life-style of the resident in the direction of personal and social autonomy. The quality of life of the resident must be of prime importance. His or her individual needs and interests must be considered. Efforts should be made to insure that all residents spend every day in as meaningful and as satisfying a manner as possible and be afforded opportunities in a wide variety of activities, within only those limitations recommended by the resident's physician.

A quality activity program in an extended-care facility should be designed to meet the following goals:

1. To alleviate the resident's fears of loneliness, abandonment, and impending death
2. To provide stimulation and pleasure
3. To discourage potential tendencies of withdrawal by encouraging the residents to share activities and experiences with their peers in group situations, thus fostering a "we are not alone" feeling.
4. To reawaken the latent skills and interests of the resident, thus helping the person to revive normal life patterns.
5. To improve the resident's self-confidence and self-respect by encouraging him or her to communicate and function more effectively, thus lessening self-pity.
6. To help the resident feel a vital part of community life by bringing members of the community into the facility to entertain, instruct, and give volunteer service and by bringing the resident into the community whenever possible and feasible.
7. To encourage the resident's sense of responsibility toward others and demonstrate that the resident can still be a useful member of the community by providing opportunities to participate in civic projects.
8. To provide a variety of activities which permit the resident to be as alert and active as his or her individual physical, mental, and emotional health permit.
9. To help the resident function at optimal physical, emotional, and social level, thus maintaining or reattaining social and motor skills.
10. To assist the resident to achieve the most vital way of life commensurate with his or her abilities and disabilities.
11. To encourage residents toward individual and group enterprise and motivation.
12. To provide rehabilitation-oriented care on a short or long-term basis to prevent further disability and to return the resident to a higher level of independent functioning in caring for individual needs and increasing the capability for independence.

RESIDENT CHARACTERISTICS AND SUGGESTED ACTIVITY MODIFICATIONS

Extended-care facilities serve residents with a wide range of diseases or disabilities, including mental retardation. As a group, residents in these facilities have a potentially significant degree of physical or mental disabilities and are unable to live independently in the community. (See chapter 4, Sociological Aspects of Aging, for a description of extended-care facilities.)

The general feelings of dispair, apathy, and loneliness experienced by extended-care-facility residents is accompanied by a loss of privacy and independence. Such feelings and losses contribute to the resident's passivity and lack of motivation. Although these residents, as a group, are very heterogeneous, there are certain common characteristics of this population that may limit activity participation. These include balance and mobility problems, visual/hearing losses, digestive and elimination problems, circulatory complications, slowness of physical and mental responses, and being bedfast.

Balance and Other Mobility Problems

1. Handrails around recreation areas, especially outdoors, and in corridors are advisable. If distances between facilities are great, chairs for resting should be provided at regular intervals. In addition, because many residents may bruise easily, all obstructions should be eliminated. Area rugs and wax should not be used on floors.
2. Residents with balance and mobility problems should be provided with activities that do not require a great deal of standing or moving in a standing position. When standing/moving activity is programmed, it should include frequent periods of rest in a sitting position.
3. Because many residents may rely on wheelchairs or walkers for mobility, walkways and table heights in activity areas must be adequate to accommodate these devices. If the resident is in a geriatric chair equipped with a tray, game and craft items can be placed on this tray.
4. Activities can be modified to permit participation in a sitting position in wheelchairs or standard folding chairs.
   a. In a circle formation, perform modified exercises with or without the aid of music.
   b. In a circle formation, use a beach ball for bouncing and catching activities.
   c. Attach a bean bag by string to the wheelchair or folding chair, toss at a target on the floor or wall. The bean bag is easy to retrieve by pulling in the string.
   d. Darts, horseshoes, table shuffleboard, bumper pool, and similar activities can be performed in a sitting position. Tournaments can be organized to stimulate interest.
   e. Window gardens can stimulate interest in living and provide a motivation, or a reason, for getting out of bed in the morning.
   f. Rhythm bands, group singing, wheelchair square dancing, and other music-related activities are enjoyed by this group.

Visual or Hearing Losses

These losses occur in varying degrees and become increasingly severe with time. As reported by the National Society for the Prevention of Blindness, approximately half of the estimated 500,000 legally blind persons in the United States are 65 years of age and older, while 66% are past middle age.

1. Individuals with visual problems should be provided with large-type printed materials, including cards and other games. Magnifying devices may be helpful. Vivid colors are also effective. Good lighting is essential. If sight is insufficient for reading, recordings of books, magazines, and other materials can be played for these residents by volunteers. Braille cards facilitate participation in card games. The visually handicapped enjoy rhythmic instrument activity, singing, discussion groups, dancing, and similar activities. Many individuals with visual problems can still enjoy crafts that they learned before they developed visual problems. Basketry and other crafts uisng large-sized materials can be mastered by individuals with limited sight.

2. Individuals with hearing losses should be given instructions in small, compact groups with the speaker enunciating clearly and looking directly at the person being addressed. When large group functions are scheduled, a microphone or similar device should be used. Earphones may be effectively used with TV, radio, or stereo equipment. Rhythmic vibrations can be picked up by the resident if the sound source is placed on the floor and shoes are removed.

3. A multisensory approach is effective with residents suffering from visual or hearing losses. The use of a combination of visual, auditory, and kinesthetic cues can facilitate participation by compensating for loss of function of some sensory receptors.

Digestive or Elimination Problems

In addition to a well-balanced diet, regular exercise can stimulate proper body functions. Because these problems can exist in various forms, toilet facilities should be located adjacent to activity areas.

Circulatory Problems

Regular exercise will stimulate circulation and help the individual feel more comfortable. In addition, proper air circulation and properly controlled heat and air conditioning are essential.

Slowing of Physical/Mental Responses

1. The slowing of physical and mental responses in many individuals poses special problems for the activity recreator. Quickness to fatigue and a slowing down of body movements may necessitate scheduling only brief periods

of strenuous activity followed by quiet activity. The ambulatory resident can participate in a wide variety of activities if they are modified to decrease intensity.

2. A shortening attention span and poor immediate memory may necessitate repeating verbal instructions and demonstrations. In addition, activities may be more effective if they are scheduled for only short periods of time.

3. Frequent reminders of scheduled activities may be necessary. Scheduling of recreational activities should not conflict with nursing care and other medical treatment. Immediately after lunch and in the early evening, after dinner, are usually effective programming hours.

4. Very simple activities are necessary for residents who are severely disabled mentally. Simple rhythmic activity, singing, simple crafts, simple repetitious exercises, and parties or similar events may be enjoyed by these residents. See chapter 5, Therapeutic Intervention, for additional suggestions.

5. In Down's-Syndrome residents, the aging process occurs early and the mortality rate increases rapidly after age 40. But the cause of death tends to be identical to that of the normal aging population. This segment of our population has been severely neglected. As a group they are well below the poverty level, frequently have no children to support them, no pension plan, and very low Social-Security coverage. Because of these factors, they usually spend their later years as charity residents in state and federally supported extended-care facilities. These residents enjoy simple activities and respond exceptionally well to simple rhythmic activities and group singing.

6. The resident who is severely impaired physically but has no mental disability will need more sophisticated programming, including intellectual discussion groups, quality entertainment, and complex games and crafts adapted to the physical limitations.

7. Motivation for activity is frequently necessary. The personality of the activity leader can be a critical factor in motivation. (See chapter 8, Staff—Professional and Volunteer, for motivational techniques.)

Bedfast Patients

Bedfast patients also require recreation and activity, but all self-care and recreation equipment must be brought directly to the bed.

1. Good activities include table games such as bingo and checkers; simple crafts; modified exercises, including isometric exercises for all muscle groups, to stimulate circulation; suction darts at a board in front of the bed; socialization activities; simple rhythmic movements; musical listening.

2. An equipment cart, which can be rolled into the room, is an excellent way to expose the bedfast resident to a variety of activities.

Many of the activities included in chapter 5, Therapeutic Intervention; chapter 6, Sports and Exercise; and chapter 7, Creative Arts and Crafts can be adapted or modified for successful use with residents of extended-care facilities. An * has been placed after the activities in the Suggested Interest Inventory, pages 156-159, that may meet the needs, interests, and abilities of these residents and that can be modified to meet the diverse skill levels and potential limitations of the group.

It is important that the activities selected for individual residents be appropriate and engaged in voluntarily and not be contraindicated for their conditions. A well-organized, sensible, and realistic program, which helps maintain a normal life rhythm and keeps the resident in contact with the world at large, is essential. A variety of daily activities ranging from active to passive and formal to informal should be programmed. When appropriate, outdoor activities should be scheduled. Strenuous activities should be avoided. As with all recreation programs, the residents should be involved as much as possible in the program planning.

If the recreation program is to succeed, the recreation-activity director must cooperate with all other staff in the extended-care facility. This is an especially critical criterion when programming for residents scheduled for medication and other forms of therapy.

When programs are limited because of lack of funds or staff, an ingenious recreator can increase the scope, frequency, variety, and quality of the program by soliciting volunteers from local community organizations and schools. A frequently overlooked staff resource in extended-care facilities are the residents themselves, many of whom may possess skills and talents that the group can enjoy. If other recreation centers are located nearby, cooperative programming efforts may ease staff burdens. Or help may be available from the city or county recreation department.

The selection of activities is critical when funds and staff are limited. Art and craft activities that do not require elaborate shops or complicated equipment should be programmed. Crafts made from scraps or remmant materials, which can be secured at no cost, are excellent choices for the program. Music and music-related activities, which can be inexpensive, should be scheduled frequently because of their high-response qualities.

As with all programs, records should be kept and an evaluation system should be initiated. (Refer to chapter 9, Programming for Community Recreation Centers, Social Clubs, Retirement Communities, for detailed information on records and evaluation.)

High-quality, daily social and recreation programs suited to the unique needs, interests, and abilities of all residents can be developed in extended-care facilities if cooperative efforts of the participants, staff, volunteers, and community resources are supplemented with sound programming principles, refined by an ongoing evaluation process. The results will be ample evidence of the value of such mutual efforts.

SELECTED REFERENCES

Brown, Sally. A consultant's view of recreation services in extended care facilities. *Therapeutic Recreation Journal,* 1970, *4,* (3), 17-23.

Cannon, Kathleen Linnihan. Death and attitudes toward death—Implications for therapeutic recreation service. *Therapeutic Recreation Journal,* 1974, *8,* (1), 38-41.

Curtis, Joseph E., and Miller, Dulcy B. Community-sponsored recreation in an extended care facility. *Gerontologist,* 1967, *7,* (3), 196-199, 224.

Ginsburg, Isaiah. Therapeutic recreation: A modality for rehabilitation of the aged. *Therapeutic Recreation Journal,* 1974, *8,* (1), 42-46.

Hardie, Elizabeth A. Therapeutic recreation for the institutionalized ill aged: A rationale. *Therapeutic Recreation Journal,* 1970, *4,* (3), 9-11, 43.

Humphrey, Fred. Bibliography—Therapeutic recreation programs for the aging. *Therapeutic Recreation Journal,* 1970, *4,* (4), 26-27, 31.

Katsanis, Thomas A. Problems with activity programs in a nursing home. *Nursing Homes,* 1969, *2,* 16-19.

Littlefield, Steven R. A statewide recreation program for retarded in nursing homes. *Therapeutic Recreation Journal,* 1973, *7,* (2), 14-17.

McClannahan, Lynn E. Recreation programs for nursing home residents: The importance of patient characteristics and environmental arrangements. *Therapeutic Recreation Journal,* 1973, *7,* (2), 26-31.

McLean, Janet R. Creative recreation makes the difference between growing old and getting old. *Modern Nursing Home,* 1968, *22,* 65-67, 110.

Merrill, Toni. *Activities for the aged and infirm.* Springfield, Ill.: Charles C. Thomas, 1967.

Miller, Dulcy B. Nursing home sitting. *Parks and Recreation,* 1967, *2,* (1), 38-39, 53-54.

Mullen, Dorothy G. Recreation in nursing homes. *Management aids number 88.* Washington, D.C.: National Recreation and Park Association, 1970.

Newman, Barbara. The role of paramedical staff with the dying adult patient. *Therapeutic Recreation Journal,* 1974, *8,* (1), 29-33.

Peters, Martha, and Verhoven, Peter J. A study of therapeutic recreation services in Kentucky nursing homes. *Therapeutic Recreation Journal,* 1970, *4,* (4), 19-22.

Routh, Thomas A. Realistic recreation in nursing homes. *Therapeutic Recreation Journal,* 1970, *4,* (4), 23-25.

____. Recreation in nursing homes. *Therapeutic Recreation Journal*, 1967, *1*, (1), 3-5, 34.

Selected bibliography on therapeutic recreation service for institutionalized aged. *Therapeutic Recreation Journal*, 1970, *4*, (3), 35-37.

Tague, Jean R. The status of therapeutic recreation in extended care facilities: A challenge and an opportunity. *Therapeutic Recreation Journal*, 1970, *4*, (3), 12-16.

Thompson, Morton. *Starting a recreation program in institutions for the ill or handicapped aged*. New York: National Recreation Association, 1960.

United States Department of Health, Education and Welfare. *Federal health insurance for the aged; Regulations: Conditions of participation: Extended care facilities*. Washington, D.C.: *Federal Register*, vol. 39, no. 12, Thursday, January 17, 1974.

Walsh, Edward R. Leisure services for the institutionalized aged. *Leisurability*, 1976, *3*, (1), 8-18.

APPENDIX:
RESOURCES ON AGING

Administration on Aging, United States Department of Health, Education and Welfare, Social and Rehabilitation Service, Washington, D.C. 20201. Provides funds for service, research, and training as outlined in the amendments to the Older Americans Act of 1965.

American Aging Association, University of Nebraska Medical Center, Omaha, Nebraska 68101. An organization of scientists seeking to promote research in aging.

American Association of Retired Persons, 1909 K Street, NW, Washington, D.C. 20006. Publications: *Modern Maturity, AARP News Bulletin.* For persons age 55 or older, retired or employed. Offers educational services in the form of Institutes of Lifetime Learning.

American Geriatrics Society, 10 Columbus Circle, New York, New York 10019. Publication: *Journal of the American Geriatrics Society.* An organization of physicians interested in geriatrics.

Federal Council on Aging, Washington, D.C. Created by Congress under the provisions of the 1973 amendments to the Older Americans Act. It is an advisory to the President, the Secretary of the Department of Health, Education and Welfare, the Commissioner on Aging, and the Congress on matters related to special needs of older Americans.

Gerontological Society, 1 Dupont Circle, Washington, D.C. 20036. Publication: *Journal of Gerontology.* A professional society stressing the biological, clinical, psychological, and social aspects of aging.

Institute of Retired Professionals, The New York School of Social Research, 60 West Twelfth Street, New York, New York 12203. Pioneer organization in providing intellectual activities for retired professionals.

International Federation on Aging, 1909 K Street NW, Washington, D.C. 20006. Publication: *Aging International.* Composed of aging organizations of various nations.

International Senior Citizens Association, Inc., 11753 Wilshire Boulevard, Los Angeles, California 90036. Composed of older persons of many nations. Sponsor of the International Senior Olympics.

National Association of Retired Federal Employees, 1909 Q Street NW, Washington, D.C. 20009. Publication: *Retirement Life.* Represents the lobbies for needs of retired civil servants.

National Council of Senior Citizens, Inc., 1511 K Street NW, Washington, D.C. 20005. Publication: *Senior Citizens News.* Membership open to any age group. Represents and lobbies for the needs of the elderly.

National Council on the Aging, Inc., 1828 L Street NW, Suite 504, Washington, D.C. 20036. Publication: *Perspectives on Aging.* Provides funds under the Social Security Act, 1972 and 1974 amendments, for social services in model cities and as grants to states for services to the aged, blind, or disabled. The council is involved in research and services for the elderly and is a national resource for senior-center planning and programming.

National Institute on Aging and Center on Aging, Department of Health, Education and Welfare, National Institutes of Health, Bethesda, Maryland 20014. Provides funds for research, program projects, and training in the biomedical, behavioral, and social-science aspects of aging.

National Interfaith Coalition on Aging, 298 South Hull Street, Athens, Georgia 30301. Coordinates involvement of religious groups in meeting the needs of the elderly.

National Recreation and Park Association, National Therapeutic Society, 1606 North Kent Street, Arlington, Virginia 22209. Publication: *Therapeutic Recreation Journal.* Promotes recreational activities for the aged.

National Retired Teachers Association, 1909 K Street NW, Washington, D.C. 20006. Publication: *National Retired Teachers Association Journal.* For retired members of public or private educational systems.

Retired Officers Association, 1625 I Street NW, Washington, D.C. 20006. Represents the needs of retired military officers of the United States.

Retired Professionals Action Group, Suite 712, 200 P Street NW, Washington, D.C. 20006. An action group interested in investigative reports and class-action cases involving the aged.

State and Local Commissions on Aging. Usually located in department or office of social services in the various state departments.

U.S. Senate Special Committee on Aging, Chairman: Frank Church, D., Idaho. Subcommittee on Long-Term Care, Chairman: Frank Moss, D., Utah.

U.S. Senate Subcommittee on Aging of the Committee of Labor and Public Welfare, Chairman: Thomas Eagleton, D., Missouri.

U.S. House of Representatives Select Committee on Aging, Chairman: William J. Randall, D., Missouri.

Western Gerontological Society, 785 Market Street, Room 616, San Francisco, California 94103. Works to promote the well-being of older residents of the western states.

PURPOSEFUL PROGRAMS FOR MATURE ADULTS

International Executive Service Corps (IESC), 545 Madison Avenue, New York, New York 10022. An independent organization supported by federal and nonfederal funds to provide overseas executive service by retired executives.

Peace Corps, Action, 806 Connecticut Avenue NW, Washington, D.C. 20525. A government-sponsored program to provide overseas service for one to two years with small salaries to cover living expenses.

Retired Senior Volunteer Program (RSVP), Action, 806 Connecticut Avenue NW, Washington, D.C. 20525. Federal funds are available in public and non-profit institutions to reimburse program volunteers for travel and meal expenses.

Service Corps of Retired Executives (SCORE), Action, 806 Connecticut Avenue NW, Washington, D.C. 20525. A program administered by the Small Business Administration to reimburse retired businessmen for expenses involved in advising small businessmen.

Volunteers in Service to America (VISTA), Action, 806 Connecticut Avenue NW, Washington, D.C. 20525. The domestic version of the Peace Corps. Federal funds are available to provide small salaries to cover living expenses for one to two years of volunteer service in community projects such as work in rural slums, migrant work camps, and Indian reservations in the United States.

PURPOSEFUL PROGRAMS FOR LOW-INCOME MATURE ADULTS

Foster Grandparent Program, Action, 806 Connecticut Avenue NW, Washington, D.C. 20525. For individuals over age 60 with income below the poverty index. Volunteers are paid by federal funds at $1.60 per hour, maximum of 20 hours per week, to act as surrogate grandparents and provide affection and care to orphans, mentally retarded, physically handicapped, or troubled children and youth.

Senior Opportunities and Service Programs (SOS), Office of Economic Opportunity, 1200 Nineteenth Street NW, Washington, D.C. 20506. Intended to identify and meet the needs of persons over age 60 with projects that predominately serve and employ older persons. Projects include community-action programs to provide employment opportunities, home health services, assistance in the Food Stamp plan, nutrition, consumer education, outreach, and referral services. Whenever possible the activities are staffed by paid or volunteer older citizens.

OPERATION MAINSTREAM PROGRAMS FOR LOW-INCOME MATURE ADULTS

Green Thumb/Green Light, National Farmers Union, Green Thumb/Green Light, 1012 Fourteenth Street NW, Washington, D.C. 20005. Green Thumb programs are for men and involve them in conservation, landscaping, and other beautification by planting projects. Green Light programs are for women who are involved in such community services as aides in libraries, aides in schools, and aides in day-care centers.

Senior Aides, National Council of Senior Citizens, 1511 K Street NW, Washington, D.C. 20005. Seniors provide service in the community. Service may be provided to other older persons on a one-to-one basis in nursing homes and long-term-care facilities or in schools in the form of classroom aides or tutors.

Senior Community Service Program, National Council on the Aging, 1828 L Street NW, Washington, D.C. 20036. Community service is provided in the form of homemaking and health assistance, nutrition, institutional care, and social service administration.

Senior Community Service Aides, National Retired Teachers Association, Senior Community Service Aides Project, 1909 K Street NW, Washington, D.C. 20006. Community service is provided in the form of homemaking and health assistance, nutrition, institutional care, and social service administration.

Index